YOUR HOME YOUR FORTRESS

How to Make Any House Into Your Own Fort Knox

ઔ • ર

Bill Heid

Your Home Your Fortress: How to Make Any House Into Your Own Fort Knox
© 2011 Bill Heid

A product of Solutions From Science

Heritage
Press
Publications

Published by:
Heritage Press Publications, LLC
PO Box 561
Collinsville, MS 39325

ISBN 13: 978-1-937660-02-4
ISBN 10: 1937660028

Contents

 හ • ගෙ

CHAPTER 1

ജ•ര

BEFORE ANYTHING BECOMES OUT OF THE ORDINARY

Before Anything Becomes Out of the Ordinary

ೀ • ೧೮

Crime is a curious thing. It's a part of our daily lives. It screams at us from headlines and news broadcasts. Chances are good that we know someone who has suffered through burglaries or muggings. Yet it also manages to be an easily forgotten phenomenon unless you truly live in a "high crime" hot spot. Most of us go about our daily lives convinced that nothing will ever happen to us. Most people don't take very many precautions against crime—we simply lock our homes and our cars and hope for the best.

It's normal and natural to not want to think about worst-case scenarios. In a way it's a built-in survival mechanism. We're wired to deal with the most immediate problems in our lives, to focus on those things that we can see and understand right now. However, the tragic fact of these worst-case scenarios is that they have a way of hitting us when we are the least ready for them. Sometimes, crime victims just lose some possessions or money. Sometimes they lose so much more.

The Facts of Crime

Before you can worry about preparing for the *absolute* worst-case scenario—the coming crime wave that is going to sweep this nation before it's all said and done—you must first think about preparing for normal, every-day scenarios. What *are* these scenarios, and how can you defend yourself against them?

Here are the facts. According to the FBI:

- One property crime happens every three seconds.

6

- A burglary occurs every ten seconds. (A burglary is defined as a scenario where the criminal enters an empty home and steals what he finds inside.)
- There are 8,000 home invasions per day in North America. (A home invasion is defined as a scenario where the criminal enters the home knowing, or not caring, that someone is home; the criminal is usually armed and violent.)
- 38% of assaults and 60% of rapes occur during home invasions.
- One out of every five homes will experience a break-in or home invasion.[1]

All of this means that you have a 20% chance of going through a worst-case scenario right now. That's before anything major has happened in America. That's before the majority of the population has grown desperate.

Of course, everybody believes that *they* will always be in the 80%. People tend to offer some of the following reasons why they don't want to invest time or money in getting prepared:

- I live in a great neighborhood.
- I live in a gated community.
- I have a dog.
- I have a gun. Mr. Smith & Wesson will take care of anyone who is dumb enough to break into *my* home.

Those who fall prey to such fallacies aren't natural fools, nor are they bad people. They simply haven't taken the time to think like a criminal. If they had, they might have stopped to think about how poor their protections really are. That great neighborhood is "great" primarily because the people in them have money—it is typically *not*, in this day and age, because people have taken the time to get to know their neighbors (which could make a great neighborhood regardless of the income bracket). When people say "great" or "safe," what they typically mean is that it's not an economically distressed neighborhood. If you were a criminal, however, you'd see a normal person's version of a big-box store every time you walked into one of those great, safe neighborhoods. Your ability to afford your presence in that neighborhood is a big signal that you have things *worth* taking! And as the economy continues to decline and anger against the more affluent portion of our population tends to rise, your fancy showcase home runs the risk of being a target of spite or desperation too.

As for living in a gated community, what does that really *mean*? Typically it means that a rent-a-cop who is taking home near-minimum wage paychecks is sitting in a booth, buzzing people through. Flash anything that looks like a work badge, and you can usually get through. You can also get through with a simple bribe. Furthermore, most gated communities still have back-street entrances that allow cars to pass through. Finally, nothing at all stops a crook from parking near the neighborhood and entering its streets on foot. Sure, they're not going to take out large items that way, but if they're coming after cash, jewelry, or other small items, they can easily walk right back out of your home again. And if they're there to do you physical harm, they hardly need a truck.

Dogs *can* be good, loyal protectors and friends. However, many domesticated dogs are more likely to be curious about an uninvited guest than aggressive. Even aggressive dogs are easily put down or handled. Some criminals will simply shoot the dog. Others will throw down a raw steak laced with drugs. While dogs can be a deterrent, they're only one line of defense—not nearly enough, on their own, to defend you. You may also be surprised to learn that *big* dogs are less of a deterrent than "yappy" dogs—small, fast, aggressive dogs who are extremely territorial, unfriendly towards strangers, and *loud*.[2]

Your gun poses some problems too. If you're caught by surprise or don't have time to get to it, the gun won't do you any good at all. Home invaders typically show up armed, and even an armed confrontation with them does not guarantee that you or your family won't get seriously hurt, even killed. Home invaders also know they can get you to stand down by threatening your children or your spouse. A gun without any additional preparation to give you the advantage in a life-threatening situation won't save you.

How Bad is it Really?

Remember that our economy and our country are still in a basic state of normalcy. So how badly do you need to prepare? Just take a look at a handful of headlines.

KTVU, Oakland, CA

Search On for Suspect in Brutal Home Invasion

An armed man broke into a home in the Oakland Hills near Redwood Regional Park early Friday, robbing a family and sexually assaulting a woman...[3]

The Herald Online, Clover, South Carolina

2 Arrested After Clover Home Invasion, Fatal Shooting

Two Clover residents were arrested in connection with a Thursday morning home invasion near Clover that resulted in the shooting death of a Lake Wylie girl...[4]

Columbus Dispatch, Columbus, Ohio

Man Sentenced to 33 Years for Rape and Home Invasion

Two men, armed with a gun, broke into a duplex on Reinhard Avenue on September 27, 2008, and tied up the young couple that lived there. After ransacking the home, both men took the woman to a bathroom and raped her.[5]

It's not fun to talk about these stories or these headlines. It's not fun to look at *just* how bad the situation can really get. Unfortunately, it's necessary to understand that there are some real psychos and sickos out there. They can strike anywhere and at any time. It doesn't matter where you live in this country. It doesn't matter if you think you are somewhere safe. They strike in big cities and small towns alike. They bring death and destruction in their wake. You *need* to take steps to protect yourself.

Basic Home Security 101

Basic home security won't turn your home into a true fortress, but it will give you a slight edge. Basic home security is meant to deter the bad guys. Typically, most criminals are inclined to seek targets of opportunity—the easiest targets they can find on any given street. The methods below are meant to make your home look less attractive to thieves and to give you some basic lines of defense against a worst-case scenario.

Start by getting a monitored security system. They carry a monthly cost that's comparable to an average pizza purchase. Wireless security systems even allow you to get security for your apartment, and some equipment allows you to go without a landline phone too. Landline phones do remain the best option, however, so it might be a good idea to get a very basic phone plan, just to support the security system.

While you can install a home security system on your own, you won't get the benefit of monitoring. Monitoring ensures that someone will get the police out to your location quickly. You also get the benefit of panic buttons. Make sure you get a portable panic button on a keychain so you can keep it with you at all times. This will help you if you don't happen to be close to a security keypad if something goes wrong.

Do get a general security system warning sign. Don't use the company's sign, as it will tell criminals what system you have and, potentially, how to get around it. You don't want to give criminals that much information! You simply want to show them that your home is a bad target.

You can take this a step further by installing video cameras on your property. While things are relatively normal, video cameras represent a fantastic deterrent. The technology allows you to store the footage online rather than on-site, which means any criminal is running the risk of getting caught. Make "security camera" warning signs very prominent.

Adding security film to all of your windows will help make them difficult to break, which decreases the chances of a forced entry through the windows. Security film is affordable, and it also gives you a measure of protection against natural disaster damage. Glass is an easy point of entry—two out of three break-ins occur through glass—so you'll want to see to this detail quickly. 6 You'll also want to install simple thumbscrew-type window locks, which make it much harder for an invader to force the windows open from the outside.

Many invaders also like to simply kick down the door. Steel-core doors are much harder to force. Couple these with deadbolt locks. Do not rely on chain locks or the door locks that come on the doorknobs, which are very easy for a determined invader to defeat. These measures will at least buy you more time to call for help, to grab your gun, or to enact other security measures as necessary.

Make your home unattractive to criminals through the simple expedient of adding more light. Using timers programmed to turn lights off and on at random intervals when you're not home can give the illusion that you're there. You should also make sure to add light outside—motion detector lights are very good for this. Place them at intervals around your house that will illuminate prowlers and eliminate their hiding places. If you want to plant shrubs close to your windows, you should choose thorny shrubs that would be uncomfortable to push through rather than softer shrubs, which just provide hiding places. You can also make the approach much noisier by adding gravel around your home as well.

Make sure your yard is picked up and that you don't leave tools around for criminals to use. Ladders, in particular, should be locked up in your garage; leaving a ladder out just invites a second-floor invasion strategy. Note that in certain worst-case scenarios, you're going to mess up your yard on purpose, but you're still going to avoid leaving items that are going to be useful to intruders.

When you're not going to be home for long periods of time, ask someone to pick up your mail and your papers—don't stop them. Criminals look for signs that there is *no* activity at the house, which also includes not seeing *any* mail or papers. From your perspective, leaving *nothing* to see is as bad as leaving a huge pile of papers or mail. You should also be careful about posting a log of your activities on social media like Facebook, Twitter, Foursquare, or LinkedIn; perfect strangers can access that information and will be able to tell that you're not there to stop them from cleaning you out!

If you are home, you should put home invasion squarely into your own mentality. For example, you should have a peephole installed in your door, and you should use it. If you don't recognize the person at the door (even if it appears to just be a damsel in distress), *don't open the door*. Don't open the door if you're not expecting anyone either. You are never under any obligation to open your door, and home invaders make up all sorts of stories to gain your trust. It doesn't make sense to install a steel-core door only to open your door up so that a home invader can finish forcing his way inside! Later we'll talk about how to survive a home invasion if the worst should occur. For now, just focus on making yourself a less attractive target.

But is it enough?

The precautions we've taught you in this chapter are basic and standard. Unfortunately, they are also not enough. They almost belong to a different era, and are as outdated as an episode of *Leave it To Beaver*. They are only a start! The average American family is on the verge of living through a *new level* of crime crisis. In fact, in some parts of the country families are already beginning to live through the nightmare. You need more than basic home security—you need a fortress, and you need strategies that will help you use your fortress effectively. Read on!

CHAPTER 2

❧ • ❧

WELCOME TO FLINT, MICHIGAN

A CASE STUDY

Welcome to Flint, Michigan— A Case Study

ℰ•ℛ

It was a creepy sight—a severed, soot-covered child's doll head hanging from an electrical pole. The minor defacement, accompanied, as it was, by a toy lamb that had been apparently hung to death by an electrical wire and a toy duck similarly executed on a nearby tree, nevertheless sent shivers down the spines of the residents of Flint, Michigan.[7] Though the meaning of the vandalism was never properly teased out—indeed, the only theories were mutters about "gangs" and "warnings," the uneasy violence suggested by the images seemed representative enough of the pandemic of crime that has swept Flint's deteriorating streets ever since the auto industry began to fail. This morning residents would not only wake up to decapitated dolls but to skies darkened by arson smoke and, most likely, to the news of yet another murder.

Once upon a time, Flint had been no more dangerous than any other major city. Indeed, it had been a vibrant place, filled largely with hardworking, prosperous people. For decades, Flint enjoyed riding high and living large on the back of the auto industry. General Motors was founded in Flint. The UAW was born during Flint's great Sit-Down Strike in 1936-1937. So entwined was the auto industry of Flint that in 1945 author Carl Crow would muse: "Buick is Flint, and Flint is Buick. It is not far-fetched to say that the relationship between the city and the industry has been like that of a self-sacrificing father and a successful son. The people of Flint dug deep into the toes of their financial socks to bring the puny Buick enterprise to this community. They coddled and nurtured it through infancy and adolescence, and when it grew, Flint also grew and was rewarded with security and prosperity." [8]

YOUR HOME, YOUR FORTRESS

The housing crisis only exacerbated the decline of the auto industry, leaving behind a city that had become a hollow shell of what it once was. Flint is now the murder capital of the United States. FBI statistics also seat Flint at the head of the class for rape, aggravated assault, burglary, arson, and robbery—number one out of over 100,000 cities in the nation.[9] So what happened?

"In some ways, the story of Flint's decline is rather simple. General Motors was founded there early in the twentieth century. In time, the company's ascent drove the worker-citizens to unparalleled personal, familial, and communal gains. Job creation surged in the periods following World Wars One and Two as the demand for automobiles soared. At its peak in the 1960s, Flint was home to 190,000 persons and 80,000 General Motors jobs, and was believed to be on its way to a population of 250,000. Today, Flint's population is at 120,000 and 17,000 GM jobs remain. No one is sure if the bottom has been reached, or even if it is in sight." [10]

As the houses emptied, opportunities for crime grew. Indeed, many of Flint's vacant homes serve as hiding places for the criminal element, making the landscape ever more dangerous. The link between devastating unemployment and out-of-control inflation has made itself clear in Flint. It's not just that people are turning to crime to feed their families, which happens. The people in Flint aren't bad people. Most of them just want an honest day's work for an honest day's pay—but a lack of hope has torn the city apart.

This point needs to be driven home, not because there's any desire to excuse criminal behavior, but to make it clear that desperation could one day drive many people who seem otherwise mild and friendly to terrible acts. That is a future that you should be aware of and prepared for. It's already happened in American cities. Flint isn't the only one—it's just highly representative of a process that has taken place in other manufacturing towns across our nation.

The city's tax base has also dwindled to the point where it can barely pay to protect its citizens. Those who could do so moved away when the jobs went away, in search of better jobs and a better life. What remained were those who were lucky enough to hold on to their jobs or those who had nowhere else to go. Flint struggles with a $15 million budget deficit. Each year it is forced to lay off more police officers and more fire fighters. The city is engaged in attempting to create a plan to bulldoze entire neighborhoods, in part because it cannot control the urban blight, and in part because it can't pay to keep those areas of town safe.[11]

In 1945, a triumphant Carl Crow was studying Flint on behalf of Buick because he wanted to celebrate Flint's success. "The history of the interesting and dynamic city of Flint," he said, "has been worth the recording because it is more than the chronicle of an industrial city. It epitomizes the history of America, an impoverished little nation of farmers, fishermen, and trappers which conquered the wilderness and became great because such a large proportion of its citizens were like the men who made Flint a great industrial city. America is a thousand Flints."[12] If America is a thousand Flints, then we must learn from Flint's falter and decline just as we learned from its meteoric success. Flint provides us with a canary in the coal mine, a series of indicators that we can use to pinpoint whether or not a crime nightmare is coming to a city near you. If these factors line up, then you know that the time is ripe to defend yourself, your home, and your family—and hopefully you can do so while the resources to do so are still plentiful and freely available.

If you listen to our government, you're sure to walk away with the impression that the worst has passed. Even though they have so far generated far fewer jobs than projected, they are painting a rosy picture that unemployment is starting to fall.[13] The numbers the government report don't even cover every situation where someone might be jobless. John Williams, author of the *Shadow Government Statistics* website, pinpoints the "real" unemployment number at somewhere around 22%.[14] These are levels consistent with the Great Depression, in which U.S. unemployment rates were typically around 25%. Though people like to paint an idyllic picture of the past, pretending that things were better because there was a stronger moral fiber, the truth is that the Depression's unemployment figures sparked a crime wave in the 1930s. It could just as easily do the same as we enter our second decade of the 21st century.

The corporate tyranny—or corporatocracy*—which pulls the strings on our government and on both political parties, has little interest in reversing this trend, because it is, counter-intuitively, so profitable for them. Outsourcing jobs to Mexico, India, China, Indonesia and other countries around the world has not stopped. *The Wall Street Journal* reports that these companies cut work forces in the U.S. by 2.9 million throughout the 2000s while increasing employment overseas by 2.4 million.[15] They do this because they can usually get away with paying slave wages to the people in developing nations—wages that leave their employees without adequate food, without adequate shelter, without adequate sanitation, without adequate education for their children, and with little access to water. In developing nations it is considered acceptable to beat, harass, and abuse workers. Should the workers even think about organizing, the corporations who participate in this atrocity simply put the local governments to work for them, and the workers are murdered. Often their families are murdered and tortured along with them. Here in the United

---

* The term corporatocracy was, to our knowledge, originally coined by John Perkins, author of *Confessions of an Economic Hit Man*. Other terms have been used to describe the same phenomena—a tyranny by the corporation and rule by the corporation, rather than actual rule by elected officials who usually serve as puppets and front men for this destructive elite.

States, we are told that people can live quite well on $1.25 a day, so there's nothing to worry about. In reality, the corporatocracy has ensured that we never truly conquered slavery—we just moved it. The workers have the illusion of being able to leave, but are in fact trapped by the need to get at least a handful of food for themselves and their children. Our corporate tyranny calls this being "business friendly" and is working hard to marry the idea that such behavior is an extension of our freedom and thus vital to our patriotic vision. Often we talk about putting good people—Christians and patriots—into government positions. As we think about this, we might also think about who is really pulling the strings. It may well be time to make sure that good people—Christians and patriots—invade corporate boardrooms as well. We need people who will not tolerate slavery or other dark practices to steer the ship at all levels.

Until that happens we can expect outsourcing to continue, because most of the people steering the helms at major corporations do not have a heart for other people. They have a heart only for profit—and they've succeeded in monopolizing most of the business in our country. While a few smaller businesses have managed to thrive thanks to the Internet, there's little denying that the actions of our corporations have a profound impact on We the People. Our government is not capable of changing this course. Our government is not even interested in changing course. There is a revolving door between corporations and Capitol Hill, with the same names and faces walking in and out, trading positions every so often. Be optimistic about neighborhood efforts, community efforts, grassroots efforts, your own efforts—but do not believe for a moment that anybody in power in America right now intends to *really* do what it takes to bring the jobs back home.

The value of the dollar is decreasing nationwide, even as more and more citizens lose their means of earning an income. The price of gas now wavers between $3.95-$4.50 a gallon. This puts the price of individual transportation out of reach for many in even the middle class, at a time when there is less money to offer reliable public transportation options. Fewer people will be able to get to work at all. The price of food has skyrocketed. *Bloomberg Business* reports the price of wheat as of February 2011 was $8.40 a bushel, up from $5.54 a bushel in 2010.[16] Are your wages going up? Most people are accepting wage *cuts* to stay in their jobs; raises are growing rare and would represent far less of an increase to your standard of living today than they would have years ago. (Pick up a copy of *Rising Prices, Empty Shelves* for a more in-depth discussion on the coming food crisis and what you can do to prepare—each crisis impacts the others, creating a domino effect).

This scenario isn't just a situation which might lead to some discomfort for the people of America. It has the potential to fling us into a full-scale, third-world scenario of rampant inflation. The Fed believes inflation is "zero" because they don't "count" the cost of food and fuel, two items most people can't live without. Their plan is to print even more money.

It would be safe to say that the urban blight of Flint is coming soon to a town near you. The links between these kinds of economic conditions and high crime are well documented. One research study by the University of Ohio cites economic conditions as an even bigger factor in crime rates than police presence. According to co-author Bruce Weinburg: "Public officials can put more cops on the beat, pass tougher sentencing laws, and take other steps to reduce crime, but there are limits to how much these can do. We found that a bad labor market has a profound effect on the crime rates."[17]

The New York Times also drew a link between the state of the economy and the sharp increase in crime levels in its 2008 article "Keeping a Wary Eye on Crime as the Economy Sinks." "The last time stocks on Wall Street fell hard, in 1987, crime was exploding, and [New York] saw historic highs in murders in the following years. Before that, the fiscal crisis of the 1970s helped lead to the abandonment of neighborhoods, failing schools, and startling crime rates: robberies built through those years to a high in 1981, where there were a total of 107,495 of them for an average of 294 a day."[18]

Is it any wonder that noted trends researcher Gerald Celente advised that 2011 would be "prime time for crime time?" It's a rather simple equation. "When people lose everything and they have nothing left to lose, they lose it."[19]

Those who are prepared to withstand economic hardship, of course, will have little need or temptation to resort to crime—a fact that helps make it clear why such preparations are part of our spiritual, moral, and physical responsibilities. However, those who are prepared also become prime targets for criminals—the prepared and the lucky have what these people do not have and so desperately need. Of course, not all crimes will be crimes of need—there will be plenty of vultures who swoop in to create a culture of fear and control in the cities falling into ruin. You'll want to protect yourself from these gangs and their leaders as well.

CHAPTER 3

ೞ • ೞ

THE DAY
THE POLICE
ABANDON US

The Day the Police Abandon Us

ℰ • ℭ

The coming crime nightmare isn't a simple matter of an increase in crime. If it were, we'd simply be facing a crime wave—and not a crisis of the kinds of epic proportions that we're attempting to prepare you for. A crime nightmare such as the one we're projecting actually occurs when *two* conditions are true. The first condition is what we've discussed—a rise in crime due to unemployment and inflation. The second condition occurs when local and state governments start losing too much money to effectively mount any police defense. It's the collision that happens when too much crime shakes hands with too little protection.

Nearly every municipality and state in our union is facing some sort of budget problem right now. Most of them are faced with massive cuts across every sort of service, and police services aren't spared. Imagine how you'd feel if your county sheriff looked at you and said, "Get a gun, we can't protect you anymore?"

In some places, it's already happening.

Take Ashtabula County, Ohio. The county has lost so much money that there is but one patrol car working the entire county at any given hour. The county is only able to jail and manage about thirty criminals at a time—the ones deemed the "most" violent—while 700 or more additional criminals "await" jail time out on the streets. This scenario led Judge Alfred Mackey to issue a dire warning to his citizens: "Arm yourselves, be very careful, and be vigilant. We're going to have to look after each other."[20]

In some places, the crime isn't just "crime," but border violence and drug war spillover, as well. That's what is happening in Fort Hancock,

Texas, right now. Hudspeth County Sheriff gave the following speech to his residents when he realized he couldn't protect them from the cartel rivalries spilling over the border. "You farmers, I'm telling you right now, arm yourselves. As they say the old story is, it's better to be tried by twelve than carried by six. Damn it, I don't want to see six people carrying you."[21]

While Ashtabula County and Fort Hancock are two of the most extreme cases, you won't have to look very far to find evidence of a dwindling law enforcement presence across all fifty states. In some cases, there are simply fewer cops to handle more cases. In other cases, it's the training that's suffering—at times the training that is most vital. Ethics, basic legal training, and instruction on the proper use of force—all of the things that allow the police force to be good citizens and not just thugs with guns—are all falling by the wayside, according to a report by *USA Today*.[22]

Get Armed, Equipped, and Trained

Don't wait for the county sheriff to tell you he can't protect you any longer. Get guns now, and learn how to use them. Make sure they are well stocked and hidden around your home, as guns are a valuable target for thieves of every stripe. You'll need to get comfortable with developing the routines that can keep your home safe. You also need to consider your car as a mobile piece of your fortress by considering car safety over the long run. Chances are you will still need to move around and even do some very normal activities during a crime nightmare, just as the residents of Ashtabula County and Fort Hancock do—and just as people have to do in third world countries all over the world right now. This point was driven home by Fernando Aguirre, a survivor of Argentina's economic collapse of 2001, who wrote some very eloquent accounts of his experiences. Specifically, he addressed the issue of crime and surviving the problem of rampant lawlessness in the streets:

"After [the crap hit the fan] in 2001, only the most narrow-minded, brainwashed, butterfly-IQ-level idiots believed that the police would protect them from the crime wave that followed the collapse of our economy. A lot of people that could have been considered anti-gun before ran to the gun shops, seeking advice on how to defend themselves and their families. They would buy a .38 revolver, a box of ammo, and leave it in the closet, probably believing it would magically protect them from intruders.

Oh, maybe you don't think that firearms are really necessary, or your beliefs do not allow you to buy a tool designed to kill people. So you probably ask yourself, is a gun really necessary when [the crap hits the fan]? Will it truly make a difference? Having gone through a [crap-hitting-the-fan] scenario myself, total economical collapse in the year 2001, and still dealing with the consequences five years later, I feel I can answer that question. YES, you need a gun, pepper spray, a machete, a battle axe, club with a rusty nail sticking out of it or whatever weapon you can get ahold of."[23]

The author of this post recommends handguns, because it is far easier to carry around a handgun during your day-to-day life than it is to carry a rifle. He also stresses the fact that the high-crime scenario of a widespread economic collapse isn't like being in a war or playing soldier. He suggested common-caliber weapons and body armor as "musts." Begin pricing these items, stocking them in your home, and learning to use them right away. You don't want to simply have them lying around, waiting you for you to attempt to figure out what to do with them during a stressful situation.

Author and survivalist James Wesley Rawles puts it this way: "Tools without training are almost useless. Owning a gun doesn't make someone a 'shooter' any more than owning a surfboard makes someone a surfer. With proper training and practice you are miles ahead of the average citizen." [24]

As a side note, even in some of the dire scenarios we've already discussed you can't just go shooting people who look like they might be threatening you. You'd still have to deal with the law, and the law has specific demands for what constitutes reasonable force. Fernando Aguirre had a lot to say about the sort of "Rambo Mentality" that permeates the survival community and how it influences the choice of firearms. It's repeated here due to its simple poignancy and good common sense:

"Don't prepare for an idiot shooting a rifle at you from 200 yards away. Prepare for the sneaky son of a gun that waits until you are distracted, fed the dogs some nice pills, and gets to you when you least expect him. THAT is much more likely than someone attacking you from 200 yards away.

I didn't mean it as an insult to anyone. I'm well aware there are cases of people shooting enemies a thousand yards away. That is war. Killing someone who wants you dead before he gets close to you is perfectly logical.

Please name me one case of self-defense where the person shot the bad guy one hundred yards away.

I had a guy try to steal my car a while ago while visiting a friend at his farm. I saw the guy next to my car about 300 meters away. I had my FAL PARA with me because we were going to spend some time shooting that morning. I could have shot that guy from a safe distance, right? But you can't do that in real life. People that shoot others 300 meters away for no reason, claiming self-defense, are called psychos. I had to fold my rifle, hide it under my coat, walk to where my car and the guy were, and ask him what he wanted. When he said that he was there to take the car, I leveled my FAL at him, and as it usually happens in real life, the guy almost pissed his pants and left, babbling some BS story I no longer remember.

If someone starts shooting at you from 300 yards away, then you shoot back in self-defense; but it rarely, if ever, happens.

Any bad guy that has survived through puberty will be smart enough to get close, very close, maybe when you are distracted with some chore/fieldwork and point a gun at you, asking you to calm down and walk into the house. No way you can know what a man's intentions are 200 yards away, unless he starts shooting at you like an idiot."[25]

The truth is, you'll find a lot of different opinions about which firearms and weapons you should own. People who like guns are happy to talk for hours about the different types of weapons. A suggested shopping list, in general terms, is below. It is more important to get prepared than it is to get hung up over the advantages and disadvantages of various firearms. If you have them, know how to use them, and have enough ammunition for them, then you are light years ahead of most of the citizenry. Once you've secured this list, you can think about any other more "warlike" or "warzone" guns that strike your fancy.

- Handgun. Own a handgun for all of the reasons previously mentioned. You can hide a handgun under your clothes, take it with you wherever you need to go, and pull it out for quick use. The .40 or .45 caliber handguns are among the most effective types that you can purchase.
- Hunting Rifle. A hunting rifle can help in the "home under assault" scenarios that we'll be discussing during periods of rioting and looting. It can also help you put meat on the table in the event that there is

a food shortage, making it a good dual-use tool and a good use of your money.

- Pepper Spray Gun. A good 17% pepper spray gun (not a small handheld bottle of mace or pepper spray) can earn you time to get to safety or even drive off some attackers without putting you in the position of having to kill them. It is also an effective weapon to hand to those who might not be mentally prepared to take a human life (such as, with proper training, your children). This type of pepper spray will drive off a full-grown bear. Gel or streaming spray guns have a range of up to twenty-five feet.

- Air Horn. A sudden loud, unexpected noise can cause an attacker to leave you alone. It can also let others know that you're in trouble and might bring help, especially if you live in a tight-knit community where you know your neighbors and have many friends. This is the same principle behind the reason why you'd want to go ahead and keep an alarm system in your home, even if there isn't adequate police protection in your area.

- Knife. A good knife can save your life and assist in a close-range struggle. One that can fold and be opened at a touch would be particularly helpful in this scenario. Knives are also simply a useful tool in general and are advantageous due to this fact.

- Lighting. Motion-detector lights were already discussed in Chapter 1. Criminals still won't like light any better even if law enforcement is not able to do its job any longer because it gives *you* a better chance to shoot them. If the power is out, you might want some high-power battery-operated spotlights, LED lights, flares, or other lights that you can use to quickly illuminate an area. Light alone will scare off some criminals.

- Body Armor. You can find body armor at military surplus stores. Look for Class II concealable body armor for now, as you can always upgrade later. This is something you can wear while going to and from work during a high-crime scenario, for example. It can save your life in the event that you do wind up in some kind of firefight. It can also be invaluable in even darker scenarios where you really do have to start treating your home like a kind of military target.

- Surveillance Devices. Since most criminals will prefer to sneak up on you and your home, hide themselves, and take you by surprise, your home could certainly benefit from hidden cameras and microphones. You should be able to monitor the devices from some common area of your home. Nobody's going to be able to watch them 24/7, but if they are out in your living room or dining area where your family is spending a lot of time, they can offer an early-detection or early-warning system that could save your life.
- Silent Weapons. A bow or crossbow carries several advantages. They are completely silent. They can be used for hunting as well as for fending off attackers. Furthermore, if you can learn how to make them, the ammunition for a bow can be far more easily replaced than the ammunition for a handgun, which may or may not be available at any given time during a prolonged or extended crisis. Remember that silencers for your guns are illegal.

All of this is in addition to being able to secure your most basic needs. It goes without saying that having adequate food and water is going to be extremely important to any self-defense plan.

It's also important to note that the purpose of this list is not to prepare you for every single survival scenario out there. At times, getting prepared for different things that can happen can be overwhelming. You can find yourself trying to figure out everything from how to live on the land on the run, how to live like our ancestors did a hundred years ago, and how to make sure you have every possible thing you might need should it no longer be available. Starting with likely scenarios that are close by and "smaller" (such as a decrease in police presence and an increase in crime) is less overwhelming and easier to accomplish than trying to prepare for every possible scenario at once. You can then build up to some of the darker and more difficult scenarios over time. That is why this book is structured the way that it is—to take you through your preparations in a logical progression. The truth is, you cannot prepare for the absolute worst-case scenario until you are prepared for the "in-between" scenarios, so it just makes sense to handle it this way. Think about it—if you aren't prepared to survive a seventy-two hour emergency, then can you be prepared to survive a three-year melt down? Take it a step at a time and make preparations as you can.

Develop a Crime Nightmare Mentality

Your mindset is actually the most important part of any scenario. There are two things you'll need to watch out for. The first is developing the *will* to survive a high-stress situation like the coming crime nightmare. The second is developing mental ^{skills}, such as alertness and threat assessment. The mental skills don't require any special equipment, but they can save your life. In fact, having the mental skills to survive a crime nightmare—a crime nightmare mentality—can be a quicker route to saving your life than all of the equipment, guns, or fortifications in the world. You also need to develop a series of habits that can help you stay safe.

Let's start with developing the will to survive. Some very good emails went out from the SurviveInPlace.com course website. One of them detailed some very telling information about how the will to survive a stressful scenario can change everything:

> *"Back in the 80s, there was an incident where an F-16 pilot needed to make an emergency landing and landed at an abandoned airstrip in Alaska.*
>
> *He landed perfectly. The plane was unharmed, and he was*

fine. Unfortunately, he thought that his distress signal did not get out, and gave up, pulled out his Beretta, and shot himself.

They estimate he did this within thirty minutes of landing.

Help arrived within two hours of the initial distress call, which would have been well before his water, food, or any other supplies ran out.

This is a common story. In wilderness situations, people often die after a single night of "exposure" at fifty to sixty degrees, even when they have proper clothing. Soldiers who have watched too many movies have died in Iraq and Afghanistan after receiving otherwise non-lethal injuries.

On the other side, one of the more amusing survival stories is of a gentleman who crashed his plane in a desert area and survived for almost a week in extreme heat/cold with almost no supplies, skills, food, or water.

The driving force for his survival?

He was in the middle of a divorce and refused to die and let his wife get everything."[26]

Decide, right now, that you not only *want* to survive the coming crime nightmare, but that you *can*. Decide what is going to keep you from giving up when things get scary. The landscape may begin to look very unfamiliar. It may appear to be quite different from the things you have grown up experiencing and believing to be in your future. If you allow depression, anxiety, or negativity to take over, then you will not be equipped to use and master the mental skill set that you will need to effectively use any tools that you may purchase, either for the defense of your body or the defense of your home.

Alertness is especially important during a crime nightmare. Criminals look for times when you will not be aware of your surroundings. They like to strike when people are entering or leaving their home and then attempt to force you back into your home, where they can do with you what they will. There will be no safe times, but it's also going to be especially important to stay vigilant after dark, when the criminal element thrives. More advice from Argentina makes this clear:

> "If I could give one piece of advice concerning [crap-hitting-the-fan] security, it would be: eyes and ears wide open when you enter or leave your home. If possible, keep a gun on hand while doing either one. If something looks, even 'feels' strange, then go around the block and check again, carefully. If you see them still there, either call the police (if still available) or get help. If you approach the house with a large group of people, they will leave."[27]

Alertness will tell you if someone is following you home. Alertness will also tell you if you're being approached while you're out in public. Threat assessment will tell you what you need to do in the face of the information that alertness has given you, such as recognizing that you need to go around the block again instead of racing to enter your home.

There's also a sort of mental toughness that you'll have to develop. It's good to have Christian compassion for those who are in need, but you need to develop a mindset that lets you know that you don't owe anything to the people who might try to harm you and your family. If someone tries to stand in front of your car to make you stop so that they can rob you, for example, you should be prepared to simply gun the engine. Let them leap out of the way—don't feel an obligation to preserve their lives or limbs at the expense of your own.[28] In a scenario like this, it won't just be people after money or valuables—the worst sorts of animals will be prowling about, and they are unlikely to stop at your valuables when taking your life can be done so very easily.

Keep everything closed and locked at all times, from your car doors and windows to the doors and windows of your home. You should only have them open if you're using them to get in or out. Be wary of strangers, even if they seem to be asking you for your help, and even if they have innocent intentions. You'll have to decide who you want to interact with on a case-by-case basis.

Hiding Your Guns and Preparing Your Home

Guns are a primary target for criminals. They are valuable. They have a high barter or trade value no matter what the scenario is. And, of course, criminals can use them for themselves to commit more crimes. In some of the more advanced scenarios we'll be discussing, you will have to hide your guns from government officials too, and not just the criminals who will want to steal them.

Therefore, at this stage of the game you're going to be creating hiding places in your home. As you grow your arsenal of weaponry, you can tuck each one of them away. The hiding places may also be useful for other survival items or valuables. This serves as a secondary line of defense. If someone gets into your home while you're away, you won't lose everything if they can't find everything.

The Panic Room or Safe Room

This is also the point in your preparations where you're going to build a panic room inside of your home. It is worth noting that at least one gun should be hidden away in the panic room, but it's not really a place for a shoot-out. You'd store something like that there in case your panic room defenses fail and an attacker gets in anyway. For the most part, however, a well-designed panic room should keep you from ever having to get into a confrontation with a criminal intent on entering your home and causing you harm.

"The idea of a safe room is that in case of a home invasion (for whatever reason) you have a fortified sanctuary you can retreat to and use to summon help. It's not to bunker down and have a shoot-out; it is where a smaller, weaker (or unarmed) person can be safe while waiting for reinforcements to arrive. In one sense, it's so you don't have to have a shoot-out between you and an intruder. In another, if the intruder does break through the room's defenses, it is pretty cut and dried that it was self-defense, even in states with a duty-to-retreat statute."[29]

It's possible to build a panic room without owning your own home. It's possible to do it without spending a lot of money. How you do it will depend on your specific circumstances, so you will have to be creative and think things through. You might not be able to put together the perfect panic room, but every step that you take towards having one at all will make you safer in the event of an attack. The room does not have to be hidden. It does not have to be a conspicuous steel box. In fact, if a regular person who has entered your home can't figure out exactly where you or your family will be running, so much the better.

Evaluate the rooms in your home. Usually you're going to be using one of the bedrooms. Choose one with the least amount of interior wall space that would be available to hack through with an axe. You can reinforce the remaining interior wall surface. Most attackers won't go to those lengths, by the way, and if you're in an apartment or a home you don't own you won't be able to add a steel-reinforced wall. However, you could reinforce the interior walls by adding heavy furniture or bookshelves directly in front of the wall. Those could even be bolted to the floor, making them difficult to tip over, if you are in a situation where it is permissible to do so. It's also worth noting that you could shoot an attacker several times over in the amount of time it takes him to go hacking through a wall with an axe. They are much more likely to try to go through doors or windows. This also has to do with the mindset of the criminal who might be attempting to come after you.

Install a solid core door in your chosen room. This is the same sort of door you should have already used on every exterior door of your home. You're going to make this installation change for the same reason—it's harder to kick, punch, or shoot through a solid core door.

Upgrade the door frame so it can withstand even more force. You should also use this technique on your exterior doors now that you're upgrading your home for an even higher level of crime.

"What he doesn't know will hurt him. With a little extra work, the bracing can be hidden behind the door frame's internal molding and will not be noticeable from either inside or outside. For the burglar, that is like unexpectedly hitting an invisible wall.

...Most door frames are made of one-inch pine, which saves the contractor money. This makes them vulnerable to this basic assault. Multiple locks and bracing under the molding make this kind of entrance unlikely and will not destroy the beauty of your home.

Bracing: Take between a two- and three-foot piece of flat steel stripping (1/2 X 2 inches is good) and drill a staggered series of holes down its length. When you take the interior molding off the door in most houses, you will see the 1 x 6 (or 1 x 5) pine plank of this doorframe. That is nailed to the 2 x 4 studs of the wall (you may or may not be able to see the studs because of the drywall, but they are there).

…On the inside wall where the molding was, position the steel strip so that all the lock strike plates are behind it and its edge is along the edge of the 1 x 6. Screw it into place with long screws – leaving a few holes open. The staggered drill pattern should result in the screws seating into both the 1 X 6 and the 2 X 4 studs. Take the molding and shave or chisel the thickness off the metal strip in the proper place. Replace the molding, using the remaining holes to tack it down over the strip. Putty, and repaint."[30]

Don't get overwhelmed. If you're not a handyperson, you could, and probably should, get a door contractor to make some of these changes for you. Choose one that you trust, however, as this person will know an awful lot about your personal home defenses.

1. Add additional locks. Use outdoor quality door locks, a door bar, floor bars, foot locks, dead bolts, and additional chain bolts. You could even use an automatic locking keypad. Every lock reinforces the door and provides another deterrent. Locks which help secure the door directly into the doorframe are especially useful.31 You might consider equipping your safe room with Fenix Heavy Metal locks. These heavy-duty locks have deep channels that allow you to add a padlock and render that padlock completely immune to bolt cutters. They're also so strong that they're unlikely to break under pressure. Several of the models are better for securing outdoor spaces, sheds, or gates, but the 8" Security Bolt model could easily be installed inside your safe room door, allowing you to throw the bolt and secure it with a padlock from inside.

2. If at all possible, it's best to place your safe room in a windowless room. However, this is not always possible. It's just as likely that you'll

be using one of your own bedrooms. If that's the case, then your windows need special attention.

First, if you have a second floor, you should make your safe room a room on the second floor. This of course makes your window far less accessible. And whether your window is on the first floor or the second floor, you'll want to plant a cactus, rose bush, or other thorny plant directly beneath it.

Next, you'll want to make the window more difficult to get through. We've already suggested a shatterproof laminate as part of your early threat level security set up. For your safe room, you should add some additional protection. You can install interior aluminum rolling shutters with a heavy-duty lock to secure that portion of your room or an interior lattice or interior lockable gate such as the ones available from the Anvil Shutters Company. You might also consider heavy-duty curtains. Either solution should be designed to keep your attacker from seeing inside of your safe room, as his blindness will provide a significant advantage to you. If your attacker is trying to get in or shoot through the window, position yourself directly beneath the window so that his bullets will angle past you.[32]

3. Next, you need to stock your safe room. Your first order of business is to add a cell phone that will always stay there. If you want to make sure you have a back up for two separate situations, you can make sure it is equipped with a landline phone as well. Most phone lines are buried underground these days, so there's little chance of the lines being cut, but you could be without power, or your cell phone could be out of service. In normal circumstances, you'll be using the phone to summon help, even if the police presence is low or non-existent. Stay on the line with 911 to make sure that you keep a running log of evidence and to avoid feeling quite so alone. If there is no 911 in operation then these preparations are moot, but your phone could

still be useful for summoning a posse of neighbors and friends if it comes for that. Yes, there may be some circumstances where the phone won't be at all helpful, but you should have one anyway.

Next, you might consider making the safe room the center of the surveillance measures we've already spoken about. If you've got your video cameras and your hidden microphones running to a feed that enters your safe room, you'll be able to see and hear everything that's happening. This will again give you a tactical advantage. It will give you advance warning should you need to escape your home for any reason (if, for example, your attacker decides to set the home on fire). And it will provide a source of evidence for the day the matter winds up in court.

If the power is cut, you'll want some battery-operated lanterns in your safe room. You don't want to be operating in the dark for both physical and psychological reasons.

Finally, you should have at least one firearm in your safe room, kept in a locked safe. You'll have plenty of time to unlock it and get it ready if you need to. This should really be a tool of last resort since the purpose of the safe room is to keep you from a confrontation, but if it's necessary you'll be ready to use it, be in a good tactical position to do so, and have good legal backing when you finally do.

It's worth noting that safe rooms can have other disaster-survival applications, as well. For example, if you live in blizzard-prone areas and the power goes out, you're advised to choose a single room of your house, close all the doors, and bundle together under the blankets. Your safe room would be a natural choice. For this reason, it's also a good idea to stock your safe room with non-perishable foods, bottled water, medications, sanitation supplies, blankets, battery-powered heaters, and potassium-iodine pills (in the event of a nuclear scenario where you might need to prevent radiation sickness). If you opt for the aluminum shutters, this room could become your haven during a tornado or hurricane as well. Add a hand-crank short-wave radio to stay informed, and you've built yourself an invaluable survival resource for any number of scenarios.

Hiding Your Guns

The purpose of hiding your guns is to secure them in the event that someone breaks into your home looking for them, but to keep them close at hand so that you can get to them if you need them.[33] This will require another round of careful thought and creativity on your part.

Start by making a list of what you have to hide. If you have only three or four guns in your possession, then you don't need to go crazy ripping out your walls and floors trying to find places for them all. Instead, you can use the places and spaces that already exist inside of your home. Some spots will need more modification than others, but it's important to use them to their fullest extent so that you don't lose the benefit of the exercise by being too sloppy.[34]

You will need some basic materials to get started. Begin with a staple gun, a drill, a strong knife, heavy-duty putty, and PVC pipes with slip on end-caps. These tools will allow you to create hiding places or to take advantage of places that are already there. You might also need other tools, such as a hammer for prying things loose or a screwdriver for screwing things back down.

You can overturn sofas and chairs and pry up the staples to reveal the hollow compartments beneath the upholstery. The staple gun will then help you return the chairs to normal once you've slipped the weapon inside. If you have very large table legs, you can use the drill to create a hole where you can store ammunition. You can hollow out books and use putty to secure the weapon inside. You can also go outside and hide guns in a PVC pipe slipped into a compost heap or flower pot.[35]

For more serious hides requiring a lot more skill, pick up a copy of Sam

Adams' *Hide Your Guns*, available from Solutions from Science. The notes in this section will get you started, but this book will teach you how to really overhaul your home and furniture to the point where you can create multiple hiding spots, ensuring that you'll always be able to hold on to at least some of your guns and other valuables in the event of a home invasion. Chances are good that you can't be home *all* the time, even if your area is in a state of emergency, and you don't want to flaunt your assets to others who might enter your home while you're preparing. Hiding your weapons is a good way to protect yourself and to turn your home into a very bad place for any criminals to come knocking. These sorts of strategies turn the old warnings about refusing to follow a lion into his den into truths, instead of creating a home that is little more than a shelter for a criminal who wants to come in and have his way with your family.

Corruption

As things progress to a certain level, you may not have to worry about the widespread lack of a police force so much as you'd have to worry about a police force that becomes more corrupt during desperate times. That's not meant as an insult to the many fine men and women in uniform across the United States; it's merely an observation on the fact that corruption rises on every level as crisis increases. And, as we've already discussed, there's a dearth of training programs that can help reduce the amount of corruption that citizens may face in the future. We're talking third-world police corruption here:

> *"Every single time a cop stopped me [in Argentina] I had to give him some money. The one I tried not to I got in trouble with. Hardly a week goes by without cops getting caught robbing at gunpoint, killing, raping, or torturing someone. Last week, a police captain in La Plata was caught after he robbed a bakery store using his issued firearm."*[36]

If you ever find yourself facing a scenario where the police cannot be trusted completely, keep the following tips in mind:

- Avoid police officers and people in uniform whenever possible. Go out of your way to avoid checkpoints and traffic stops.
- Carry a bit of cash or small, valuable items for bribes at all times.
- Be polite and respectful when talking to police, but never volunteer information.
- Have at least one friend in the police department if you can manage it.[37]

Several of these tips would also be appropriate should you find yourself dealing with a martial law scenario, as they are good tips for dealing with authority figures that aren't trustworthy but that you must navigate around.

CHAPTER 4

⅋ • ℚ

TAKE BACK YOUR STREETS

Take Back Your Streets

ဢ • ဪ

Whenever one gets to talking about any kind of disaster situation, it's very easy to forget that there are always things we can be doing to attempt to turn the disaster around and to keep it from ever occurring. Even if these efforts aren't 100% successful, they can still be very valuable exercises over the long haul. Any action that causes you to band together with your community in the hopes of creating some positive change has the effect of creating the community foundation that could save your life if the situation spins out of control in spite of your best efforts. A strategy that relies on you hunkering down in your own personal fortress to ride out the storm is always an incomplete strategy.

Make no mistake—you will need community. Those who live in smaller, close-knit communities and who get to know their neighbors are in a better position to survive any kind of crisis than those living at the other extreme of the spectrum. Here's Fernando Aguirre again:

"After all these years, I learned that even though the person that lives out in the country is safer when it comes to small time robberies, that same person is more exposed to extremely violent home robberies. Criminals know that they are isolated, and their feeling of invulnerability is boosted. When they assault a country home or farm, they will usually stay there for hours or days torturing the owners. I heard it all: women and children getting raped, people tied to the beds and tortured with electricity, beatings, burned with acetylene torches. Big cities aren't much safer for the survivalist that decides to stay in the city. He will have to face express kidnappings, robberies, and pretty much risking getting shot for what's in his pockets or even his clothes.

So where to go? The concrete jungle is dangerous and so is living away from it all, on your own. The solution is to stay away from the cities but in groups, either by living in a small-town community or subdivision, or if you have friends and family that think as you do, form your own small community. Some may think that having neighbors within "shouting" distance means losing your privacy and freedom, but it's a price that you have to pay if you want to have someone help you if you ever need it. To those that believe they will never need help from anyone because they will always have their rifle at hand, checking the horizon with their scope every five minutes and a first aid kit on their back packs at all times...Grow up."[38]

An understanding of why community is so important can prepare you for understanding how crime-reduction theory works, and how you can band together with other members of your community to reduce some of the impact of the coming crime nightmare, maybe even steer the worst of it towards other communities. These strategies won't end crime entirely, and they're no replacement for the preparations we're taking you through, but they can be a very good glue that holds all of the preparations together into a single unified strategy.

Such an initiative also serves another purpose—reminding you that there is more for you to do than hunker down helplessly, endlessly fortifying your own living space in the anticipation of ever-more gruesome scenarios. Furthermore, many of the community initiatives to fight crime have been known to work—and work very well. Getting involved at the community level also helps to counteract a dangerous over-reliance on the government. Many otherwise well-meaning people support a number of intrusive and expensive government programs over community, faith-based, or charity initiatives because they don't see the latter options working to a satisfying degree. This is in part because the modern lifestyle lends itself to a hyperactivity of "busyness," from work to extra-curricular activities for the kids. If we can turn some of our attention back to revitalizing these programs and showing just how effective they can be (and just how superior to government intervention), we can go a long way towards winning back a popular support of the Republic as intended by our founding fathers. Most people want the same basic things: jobs that are available, that pay a wage that people can live on, and neighborhoods that are a safe place to raise their families. Many people want those things for others too. Be the change you want to see—be the alternative—and you might contribute to a turnaround before the situation in America gets completely out of control. We are not yet in a complete state of collapse—so adopt a here-and-now mindset and become a force for positive, voluntary change.

Broken Windows

Taking back your streets demands that you have a decent understanding of the "broken windows" theory. The broken windows theory was first developed by James Q. Wilson and George Kelling:

> *"Most criminals behave with rationality, selecting for their crimes locations they believe will offer high rewards but a very low risk of getting caught...This thesis suggests that the following sequence of events can be expected in deteriorating neighborhoods. Evidence of decay (accumulated trash, broken windows, deteriorated building exteriors) remains in the neighborhood for a reasonably long period of time. People who live and work in the area feel more vulnerable and begin to withdraw. They become less willing to intervene to maintain public order (for example, to break up groups of rowdy teens loitering on street corners) or to address physical signs of*

deterioration. Sensing this, teens and other possible offenders become bolder and intensify their harassment and vandalism. Residents become more fearful and withdraw further from community involvement and upkeep. This atmosphere then attracts offenders from outside the area, who sense it has become a more vulnerable and less risky site for crime."[39]

If the deterioration process works through broken windows and trash, then a process of reversing the trend works in the opposite manner—responsible citizens get together to take charge of the area and clean it up. A well cared-for area already represents a higher risk to criminals. In addition, the act of sponsoring, spear-heading, or joining with a clean-up force allows you to get to know your neighbors, forming the backbone of a community that will be committed to looking out for one another in a crime wave or any other crisis.

To put it another way, you are treating your community much as you would treat your home—by progressively making it a very difficult place for criminals to operate and by putting as many deterrents in place as possible.

The Seattle Police Department offers a list of items to target on their website, including:

- Quick replacement of broken windows
- Prompt removal of abandoned vehicles
- Fast clean-up of illegally dumped items, litter, and spilled garbage
- Quick paint-out of graffiti
- Finding or building better places for teens to hang out than street corners
- Fresh paint on buildings
- Clean sidewalks and street gutters [40]

Communities in such crime-ridden areas as New York City, Washington D.C., and Miami have all seen positive results from tackling these issues that seem so very cosmetic on the surface. In addition, even teenagers have successfully executed clean-up programs around their neighborhoods. While these measures aren't exactly going to stop a full-scale crime wave brought on by economic distress, they can certainly act as mitigation factors. Furthermore, if you find yourself in a position of having to ask your neighbors for help because the police aren't there to work with, you'll be better served by having an aware and partially organized group of people on your side.

Community Programs

Many good community programs already exist. There's also a lot of good guidance out there for actively starting your own community program or planning your own community clean-up project:

"A good first step is to look around at areas that need attention. Is a community park littered? Is an empty lot filled with tires, construction materials, and overgrown bushes? Is a nearby stream an eyesore that discourages people from enjoying it?

Look at the people in your group. What skills do they have? Picking up trash and mowing grass requires one level of skills; hauling huge hunks of concrete or using chainsaws to cut up lumber calls for another. Helping hands are the most important ingredient for a successful outcome; many of the materials and services needed can be donated by local businesses and governments, even for a major community spruce-up.

Create partnerships. Joining up with another neighborhood or community group can build your group's credibility and provide more help to get the work done. Environmental groups, civic associations, the local recreation and parks department, business associations, service clubs, and religious and social groups my be able to help or suggest other groups."[41]

Before you start organizing, however, you should check out the groups that are already formed in order to save time and energy and to avoid working at cross-purposes with those groups. Try looking for a Partners Against Crime Program, Citizens Against Crime, or a Neighborhood Watch. Neighborhood Watch groups, in many areas, have extended their scope far beyond peering out windows and notifying local police, and they're quietly more effective than simple street signs.

"Neighborhood Watch—this most widespread crime prevention effort in the United States has a long track record of success. It is so well-represented that major criminologists do not generally undertake studies of whether it works—just how it works.

Successful Neighborhood Watch programs move beyond the basics of home security, watching out for suspicious activities, and reporting them to law enforcement. They sponsor community cleanups, find solutions to local traffic problems, collect clothing and toys for homeless families, organize after-school activities for young people, help victims of crime, tutor teens at risk for dropping out of school, reclaim playgrounds from drug dealers, and form task forces that influence policymakers. They can even start a safe house program for children or a Block Parent program, which are reliable sources of help for children in an emergency or other frightening situation. After a number of natural disasters in the Midwest, Neighborhood Watch groups there have designated Family Emergency Preparedness plans. The scope of Neighborhood

Watch continues to grow, however, its fundamental mission still remains—people helping people."[42]

Since crime-prevention programs tend to work hand-in-hand with police departments, you'll be achieving another end as well. Earlier we discussed the fact that you might want to have a good friend in the police department in the event of widespread corruption. Finding that honorable friend right now, while corruption is low and while you're more certain of who you can build trust with, will be a lot easier if you're involved in meeting working police officers out where they are. Again, this is a matter of preparation. A Neighborhood Watch could form the backbone for something much greater, even a community patrol that keeps banditry at bay once everything falls apart, but it won't be able to accomplish anything if you're trying to scrape up support and leadership for it after the fact. It will be much harder to get a demoralized and blindsided population to work together than it will be to use connections that you already have, connections with people that are already accustomed to being proactive. This "survival network" also means that you don't have to risk yourself by being too free with your views or by attracting the attention of the state or local government just because you've tried to join a group of more obviously like-minded individuals. These programs have good reputations and have been going for decades.

If you do find yourself in the position of having to take on a full-on citizen's crime action network (prior to the point where there just aren't any police to work with) you can ask for the police to help you. You can even create citizen's patrols that wear brightly colored caps or special t-shirts (uniforms). These patrols typically walk the neighborhood, writing down the license plate numbers and descriptions of people who are engaged in suspicious activities, taking photographs and videotapes and passing them to the police. Criminals quickly become aware that this sort of evidence gathering is going on and quickly find other places to work. This kind of action might also involve you demonstrating against landlords who rent property to drug dealers or businesses that sell drug paraphernalia like marijuana rolling papers.[43] If there ever is a total breakdown of law and order (such as after a major nuclear crisis, EMP event, or war event) this very group could potentially be armed and organized into a citizen's police force with very little effort. If the police ever abandoned us, this group could be formed into a phone-tree, and they can show up at your house armed, ready, and in large number, should you call them from your safe room. Criminals will be more likely to leave when faced with such a group then to engage in any sort of protracted shoot-out, and if they know such a group already exists, they may be prone to watch for people who are coming.

Citizen and community action may seem unbearably "fluffy" to those who have trained themselves to think primarily in terms of armed conflicts after a total disaster scenario. However, history has aptly demonstrated that people need other people in order to survive. Recent collapses and disasters have taught the same lessons. Communities that pull together after a disaster will fare better than those who are full of people riding high on a philosophy of "my family, me, my gun, and supplies." You won't be able to do a thing in this direction if you're not "plugged in" to the community in some form or fashion. And even those who are living in the sorts of suburbs or tight-knit communities described by Fernando Aguirre will have a hard time knowing who to call or reach out to in the event that they need help if they've lived as isolationists during most of their time in that community. In addition, such a person will lose their real God-given opportunity to reach out and help others. Get connected now, while it's still easy to do so.

Keeping Order in a Community after a Crisis

Though most of this book focuses on the coming crime nightmare, which is a very specific sort of disaster, there's no escaping one important fact: every disaster, survivalist nightmare, "end of the world as we know it," or collapse scenario that you can think about is a matter of a number of highly related factors. All of the unrest and unease is coming from a tapestry of sources. The fragile web of food sources, currency issues, economies, government actions, war threats, and natural disasters that allows us to spin out disaster scenario after disaster scenario all touch on each other. They are dominos waiting to fall, and what really remains is to see which direction they fall in and what challenges that fall brings. If you are dealing with the crime nightmare, it's a sure bet that it is because factors which could bring about much more dangerous scenarios are starting to rear their head.

Nobody really knows how everything will go down, though everyone seems to have his or her own sort of "pet scenario." One scenario involves the gate shutting on a deadly totalitarian society involving martial law and Nazi-era horrors. This is a scenario that we do address elsewhere in the book. Other scenarios involve a sudden shift in geo-political events that takes matters out of everyone's hands very quickly, including our own governments. These scenarios involve a major nuclear or EMP attack that quickly causes a complete failure of all banking, communication, and electrical services, which, in turn, causes a complete breakdown. Your community may well find itself in a situation where it has to solve its own problems—and fast—absent of any guidance or resources from the state or federal government. A lot of different factors will determine which communities survive and which die off, but one of them will surely be the capability of the community's members to pull together to establish and maintain some form of order should the worst occur. Again, your ability to be "connected" at all will determine both how helpful you can be to the effort as well as how likely the effort is to succeed at all. The fact that you've stopped to read this book, or other books like it, indicates that you will already have a degree of knowledge and mindset that will be absolutely vital in such dark days.

Someone will have to take up responsibility and leadership once the dust settles, and others will have to be on point and ready to help with that. History has shown that humans crave leadership and, when there is a vacuum, humans will leap forward to fill that vacuum for good or for ill. Any true defense strategy has got to include thinking in terms of leadership.[44]

Though you may not wind up the leader of your particular group, it's still important to be aware of the types of issues that leadership would have to face and where you might fit into being part of the solution rather than part of the problem. James Wesley Rawles posted a very comprehensive discussion of the various issues at SurvivalBlog.com titled *Community Crisis Planning for Societal Collapse, the Definitive Guide.* If you happen to know your own community's mayor, town council, or other members of the community leadership, it would be good to be able to go to such people armed with this information. If you *are* such a leader, then you will definitely want the information. If such leaders have fled or been killed in the initial stages of a crisis, you might need to "step up" and become that leader, or someone in your community-action group might. This is all the more reason to get into the habit of taking action right now, and taking responsibility for an area of protection outside of your own door.

Think of it this way: Any protection plan is built in layers. If one item of the plan fails, there's always the next layer. Getting involved at the community level is the outermost layer of your plan—an invisible "wall" that you're constructing. It may encompass, say, fifty homes. If the criminals are bold enough to work past that wall, you have all of the home and self-defense techniques you've already been building to protect your home and your person until help can arrive or until the criminal is driven off. While it's good to know how to live off the land and hide in a tent for months at a time in the event of this level of horror, that should be a plan of last resort and not a plan of first resort. A good plan of first resort would be to have many others around you committed to mutual protection—that is why walled towns and communities first sprung up in the ancient days to begin with, and why wandering families and clans eventually consolidated themselves into large fortified cities later.

CHAPTER 5

❧ • ❧

CASE STUDIES

RIOTING AND LOOTING

Case Studies— Rioting and Looting

ଚ୍ଚ • ଚ୍ଚ

It doesn't take a major period of disaster to spark a riot. Such behavior has happened as a result of sports games, jury verdicts, and other more minor issues. This only proves you don't need to see an "end of the world as we know it" scenario to begin thinking about how to protect yourself in the event of things going wrong. However, it also doesn't take a genius to see that riots and looting go hand and hand with most major situations, from earthquakes in Haiti to major food riots around the world as prices skyrocket.

Therefore it is vital to understand these events as part of an overall pattern of crime, and to think about how you might deal with such events should they disrupt the peace of your local area and threaten your family. In Chapter 6 you will learn specific strategies for protecting your home and family from these dangerous outbreaks of violence.

In some situations you'd be facing riots born out of anger, feelings of helplessness, or a sense of oppression and fear. In others you'd be faced with a snatch and grab for vital supplies. In other cases you'll be dealing with a combination of both.

Danger Signs of a Boiling Pot

Often, when people talk about defending their homes against looters, they are thinking only of sort of potential total meltdown scenario. Yet people in the United States have had to defend their homes against looters before. There are four major danger signs that would indicate that riots could become a problem.

The first is a sense of anger or dispossession. Tens of thousands have taken to the streets of Athens, Greece. They're doing it because the government is being forced to enact harsh "austerity" measures to cover an enormous debt to the IMF and World Bank. This means that many families are simply unable to survive. Unemployment has skyrocketed to a staggering 40%, and the debt has grown to 150% of the annual economic output. Some government employees have continued to work but have waited two months for paychecks that never materialized.

"The situation that the workers are going through is tragic, and we are near poverty levels," said Spyros Linardopoulous, a protestor with the PAME union blocking the port of Pireaus. The government has declared war, and this war we will answer back with war."[45]

In the L.A. riots of 1992, it was a sense of racial oppression and a lack of voice that finally inspired the level of anger and fury that destroyed an entire city block.

"Todd Eskew, a member of the black "Crips" gang was more intent on creating victims than worrying about becoming one. He can't recall how many windows he broke, or how many fires he and his friends started. They'd light anything in a store that would burn and spread flames quickly and then run. Their rage was born of poverty and humiliation, and years of perceived abuse by police and neighborhood Korean stores.

"I was so angry I wanted to continue. But I stopped after two days out of sheer, physical exhaustion," says Mr. Eskew, who goes by the name of Najee Ali today."[46]

It would be unrealistic to assume this level of anger and despair does not exist in the United States today. In February 2011, we saw 55,000 people rise up to protest at Wisconsin's state capitol over collective bargaining rights and austerity cuts. Though these protests did not set the capitol on fire, it could have easily devolved into a riot. America has become divided across a thousand tiny fracture lines: race against race, religion against religion, even profession against profession. Everybody is angry at everyone else, and everyone is looking for someone to blame. Those who are really responsible have, in fact, continued to profit off of their divide-and-conquer stratagem. You can expect to see many other people taking to the streets—people who are angry, even furious. Whatever you feel about their personal take on the issues, one thing is clear—it would not take much at all to turn these people into a rampaging mob intent on destroying and taking whatever they can. Trends researcher Gerald Celente appeared on Fox Business on April 13, 2011, to predict revolutions, riots, rebellions, and marches as governments try to squeeze more money out of their constituents and as more jobs dry up. This just provides further proof for the reasons why it is going to become important for you to have a plan to defend yourself against an enraged population.

Poverty, need, and a lack of supplies is the second danger sign that looting is on the way. Some people will take to looting just because they didn't (or couldn't) get prepared in the first place.

Haiti was one of the poorest nations in the world even before the devastating earthquake of 2010. Looting broke out almost immediately:

"With the people of Haiti hungry, desperate, and frustrated nearly a week after a powerful earthquake, sporadic violence and looting [was] erupting in the badly damaged capital."[47]

Similar scenes broke out in New Orleans after Hurricane Katrina. Looters were carrying out diapers and other supplies right in front of rolling television cameras. While some looters are opportunists who will make off with goods not at all related to survival, others are trying to make up for their lack. Unfortunately, functionally, the danger is the same to you, the well-prepared individual who has supplies.

Disasters create a special scenario in which looters stop fearing potential consequences. Looters know that law enforcement is likely to be overwhelmed, and that their own chances of getting rounded up are slim. The lack of fear over consequences creates the third ingredient that makes looting a surety. Once law and order breaks down on any level, it becomes immediately clear that there is nobody strong enough to stand up and stop the madness. This is, in fact, one reason why looting is likely contagious—riots in one city are likely to spark riots in other cities. The second set of rioters now has a positive model that assures them that very few of the malcontents will face any consequences for their actions.

Yet looting and rioting don't always break out, even in times of disaster. The world has watched in awe as the Japanese victims of the 2011 earthquakes made miso soup on the street and fed it to one another instead of breaking out into frenzied looting. This is in part because of strong filial bonds and cultural traditions in the Japanese people.

"John Swenson-Wright, a Japan expert at London's Chatham House think tank, believes the answer has to do with Japanese culture.

'There's a general sense of social responsibility that's very fundamental to Japan. Part of that is self-regulation on the part of individuals, part of it is a society in which people are very conscious of their reputations in the eyes of their neighbors and colleagues,' Swenson-Wright told AOL News today. 'They're reluctant to do anything that would invite criticism.'

Another factor is Japanese people's deep-rooted sense of honor, embodied in the words today of their emperor, who rarely speaks publicly and stays out of politics.

'I hope from the bottom of my heart that the people will, hand-in-hand, treat each other with compassion and overcome these difficult times.'[48]

Therefore, you can see the *lack* of strong cultural traditions of honor and decency and the lack of strong filial bonds for fellow countrymen to be real danger signs of riots waiting to happen. It doesn't take much argument to demonstrate that America lost these bonds long ago—if our culturally and ideologically divided melting pot ever had this kind of cohesion to begin with. There have always been tensions between races, religions, and classes on our shores, tensions that have erupted at various times. It would be intellectually dishonest to deny these tensions or these differences or to fail to address our failure to successfully treat all people as we ourselves would like to be treated throughout our nation's history. From the horrors wrought on Native Americans to our treatment of kidnapped African slaves, from the insults and prejudice suffered by Irish immigrants to our citizens of Japanese descent rounded up and placed in internment camps, our record, even during our strongest times of spiritual and moral fortitude, is a spotted one.

Inadequate Services

It won't take a total melt-down for police and fire services to become unavailable in the event that you become caught up in a scenario of total social unrest, even if your city or state has been able to hold on to its own manpower in the wake of staggering budget cuts. Periods of civil unrest are more than capable of completely decimating the ability of law enforcement to respond. Just listen to the voice of one Los Angeles police officer who lived through attempting to quell the L.A. riots of 1992:

"During civil unrest, 9-1-1 couldn't even help us officers, let alone someone else on the street. Communications and 9-1-1

were up and running, but they were paralyzed due to the sheer scope of the violence that was raging in the city. If mass civil unrest happens in total collapse, even the safeguards that have been thought of and put in place since those riots will not work as manpower dwindles. Do not make your plans with any sort of help regarding 9-1-1. If some comes, consider it a bonus.

…On several locations the fire captain would pull up to a strip mall and make an on-the-spot-decision whether or not the building could be saved with the manpower we had available right then. A sort of fire department triage if you will. If he didn't think he could save the buildings with what he had, they let the building burn and moved on.

…On the surviving buildings, there had been [armed] men on top of them and I observed several fired shell casings around the buildings. We chatted with those brave men and women inside their little fortresses, and they were determined to keep their businesses and property from being looted and burned."[49]

In other words, you don't have to sit back and believe in a series of unlikely Mad Max events to decide that you are the only one who is going to be responsible for defending your own home in the event of a massive event of civil unrest. All you have to do is look towards very recent history, towards events that have already happened on our own shores, to decide that you will have to take steps to defend your own home and family.

You also need to be aware that the crazies racing through the streets won't just be your average poverty-stricken citizen who gets his hands on a baseball bat. These events provide very real opportunities for prison-breaks to happen on a massive scale. In Haiti, the earthquakes allowed 4,000 convicts to escape and take to the streets. These are hardened criminals who have already proven their willingness to kill, steal, and rampage. These are the types of thugs that will be some of the most dangerous in the event of a crisis—it's about more than greed, yet people are running in to steal televisions and designer shoes![50]

Businesses First, but Homes Soon Follow

Overwhelmingly looters target businesses first, but homes do follow. In the event of a protracted crisis, business targets will dry up rather quickly, leaving homes as the only viable targets that are left. In Missouri, for example, tornado victims suffered from looters even as they tried to rebuild their homes. The looters weren't even after survival supplies— they stole power tools, jewelry, and copper piping.[51]

Tornado victims wound up fighting off looters with crowbars in Monson, Massachusetts, in order to keep them out of their homes.[52]

If you had visions of not having to worry about looters because you do not own a business, or if you'd imagined that looting would be confined to Wal-Marts and 7-11s, these terribly recent cases (June 2011) prove otherwise. This wasn't even the result of a total meltdown. Calm, life-as-normal civilization was a drivable distance from both of these disasters. And yet you see a small microcosm of what would happen all over the country if a true disaster swept our nation.

Almost a Certainty, No Matter What Happens

Since our nation shows almost every danger sign of a looting scenario waiting to happen, you can be assured that this is something you're going to have to worry about no matter what happens. It doesn't take an "end of the world as we know it" scenario. It could be wildfires. It could be an earthquake. It could be tornados or hurricanes. It could be a chemical or biological warfare attack, a nuclear plant meltdown, or a terrorist attack with a dirty bomb. It could be the slow slide of our economy, which already prompting "mob robberies" in Minnesota and other places. It could be protests against austerity. Whatever it is, you need to know how to get your home prepared for this darkest and most certain of "worst case" scenarios.

CHAPTER 6

ഔ•ര

DEFENDING YOUR HOME AGAINST RIOTERS AND LOOTERS

Defending Your Home against Rioters and Looters

ഇ • ൫

We've now established that rioting and looting follow trouble like vultures follow corpses. And we've established that you can expect this behavior in the early days of any crisis, from a massive weather disaster to worst-case events. In Chapter 4 we discussed banding together with your community to mitigate crime in a crisis, and this may still be a step you'll want to take. However, you will have to actively survive an influx of people who did not prepare for the crisis and who are after your food, water, medical supplies, weapons, and other valuables before you can worry about the community at large.

Any preparations that you do for this day will have to be done in advance of the event. You don't want to wait until the rioters and looters are outside of your door—by then it will be too late. You will need both the appropriate tools of your fortress and an appropriate plan to succeed in defending your home and family.

To this point, we've been talking about different phases of security threat and the minimums you would need to have in place to be ready for each phase. Phase 0 was the normal American lifestyle phase. Phase 1 would be the high crime waves that are being suffered in economically depressed areas like Flint, Michigan. Phase 2 would be a situation where the police can't or won't help. Rioters and looters would definitely represent a Phase 3 situation.

By now, you should have taken the following steps, or put together plans to help you take the following steps. The easy checklist below will get you prepared for most Phase 0 through 2 scenarios. You may not be able to take every single step. If you live in an apartment building, for example, you may be limited in what you will be able to install. You might not be able to put in a monitored security alarm system, but you may be able to put in "squealers" that tell you when a door or window has been opened—anything that can alert you to the fact that you're being invaded and buy you extra time. If you do own your own home, however, the must-haves are irreplaceable for protecting your family and your investment. Think creatively during the times when your own situation might not allow you to put in every security measure you might want to have.

Must-Haves

- Monitored security system
- Video cameras
- Security film on windows
- Thumb-screw window locks
- Steel-core exterior doors
- Deadbolt locks on all exterior doors
- Timed interior lights
- Motion-detector exterior lights
- Thorny shrubs planted, especially under windows
- Gravel around the home perimeter
- Ladders and other useful tools put away, out of the reach of criminals
- Peephole installed on the front door
- Weapons training
- Handgun and ammunition
- Hunting rifle and ammunition
- Pepper spray gun
- Air horn
- Knives
- High-powered battery-operated spotlights
- Body armor
- Hidden microphones
- Silent weapons, e.g. crossbows
- Hiding places for weapons
- Established safe room
- Joined or started a community anti-crime program

DEFENDING YOUR HOME AGAINST RIOTERS AND LOOTERS

Nice-to-Haves

- One small "yapping"-type dog
- One large, aggressive dog (still useful as a line of defense even if you are not using the dog as a primary deterrent)
- Live in a gated community
- Own additional weaponry, including shotguns and assault rifles

If you've taken all of the above preparations, you're now ready to begin creating a plan for a situation where rioters and looters might be a threat.

At this point you might want to consider installing a tall wrought-iron fence with spiked decorative tips around the perimeter of your yard. Make it something that's too difficult to jump or climb safely without leaving the possibility that your attackers could get hurt. A good steel gate should be lockable, and you can use one of the Fenix Heavy Metal locks to make it less vulnerable to bolt cutters. Such a fence offers the invaders no privacy, creates fewer routes of fast escape, and makes your house a lot less attractive to all manner of criminal types. The fence would also slow down a large group of intruders long enough to shoot them down if necessary.[53]

Some of the bottom feeders that might be coming after your home won't just be random people who might be deterred by your fortifications. Some will be well armed, perhaps even well trained. In this case, your fortifications will only act as a signal that you have something to protect. Your fortress home will simply strike such a person as a challenge they need to overcome. In fact, some of these people might have some training and might be aching for a chance to show off how they can overcome such challenges![54]

When looting and rioting do come, you should also be aware that it's time to "dig in." Resist the urge to go out for any reason, even if the trouble seems to start as a peaceful protest. Peaceful protests can turn into riots, especially if you're talking about a widespread, countrywide uprising in response to a disaster. You don't want to be caught in the middle of such a tide. Even if you want to be part of the effort to bring justice, you need to recognize that this is a bad time to be out on the streets, especially if you have a family.[55]

Instead, it's time to go on "high alert" and get serious about defending your home. Begin by making your house look as though it has already been targeted and picked clean. Spread trash, broken furniture, broken hardware and other debris around your yard. Looters are typically in a hurry. They are operating on a mob mentality and, if you are lucky, they may not stop to examine the scenario too closely if they believe you no longer have anything worth taking.[56]

You'll also need additional gear to be fully prepared for this scenario. You'll need:

- Pre-cut plywood or roofing metal. Make sure you've sized these to fit over any windows that have been shot out. In addition, you should make sure you've cut gun ports so you can continue to defend your family in the event of a protracted battle.[57]

- Tactical ballistic shields. These are freely available for sale over the Internet starting for around $800 and ranging all the way up to about $3000. These are the same variety that riot police use, and they could wind up being lifesavers for you too, if anyone actually breaks through your defenses and makes it into your home.

- Sand bags. You can stack sand bags up against the doors. They are capable of withstanding quite a bit of gunfire and provide extra protection against having your door kicked down or broken down.

- Less-than-lethal (LTL) ammo. Some schools of survivalist thought might disagree, but you really need to think this through. If your preparations are sufficient to keep looters outside of your home, you're not really justified in using lethal force against them. If you just want to scatter the attackers and send them on their way, you can use LTL ammo to accomplish your goal. Police use this kind of ammunition in a riot to break up a crowd, and it is good enough for your home, too. That's not to say it's the *only* sort of ammunition you should have. It is painful. It also sends the message that you are prepared and serious. If you find yourself in court after the disaster (assuming this isn't some sort of apocalyptic scenario where law and order will never again be restored), then you've shown that you used the less-lethal alternative first. Birdshot, buckshot, and bean-bag rounds would be very useful here.

- Hand-held radios. Assuming more than one person is going to be involved in the defense of your home (perhaps manning multiple windows or gun ports), you'll want a way to communicate besides shouting across the house. You won't be able to use your cell phone for this purpose as they are not likely to be reliable. The handheld units will allow you to coordinate with the rest of your team.
- Fire extinguishers. If someone tries to set your house on fire, you may be able to salvage things with large fire extinguishers before you have to risk an escape. This would also be good for small, localized fires, such as those caused by a single Molotov cocktail.
- Bug-out bag. You should have a bug-out bag anyway, of course, but in this context a bug-out bag would be specifically used in the event that someone sets your house on fire and you need to escape. That way you'll have at least a few survival essentials on hand, and you can plan your next step in better shape than if you'd just lost everything you owned to a random act of destruction.

At this point you'll have to choose how to defend your home. This means using your home to its fullest tactical advantage.

"Your best line of sight is always from up high. By taking positions in the second floor rooms, you have the advantage

over any street assault. If you don't have the second floor, you will want to position yourself as high up on your first floor windows as possible. Your gun ports should be near the top corners of your window shield."[58]

There are also some prep actions you *don't* want to take. On survival forums and in the comments on survivalist blogs, there is a lot of talk about using lethal booby traps to defend your home in the event that looters or rioters arrive. This is a bad idea for several reasons.

First, there's always the chance that lethal booby traps will backfire. If they're something you're planting in your yard, they're also something you could end up stumbling over by mistake if you're trying to escape. Since a bad situation could break out at any time, they'd have to be set before that happens—which means you could wind up with traps in your yard or home that other members of your family might set off.

Second, there are very few scenarios where some form of law isn't going to be restored after the initial crisis has passed. If you break the law while trying to defend your home, you're going to find you have bigger problems than you could have anticipated. Lethal booby traps are illegal, especially if they are rigged to any sort of firearm.

"A booby trap involving a firearm, sometimes called a trap gun, is never legal, justified, or necessary. The idea is that the firearm is rigged inside of a structure in such a way that if an intruder enters a structure, he sets off a mechanism that makes the firearm discharge.

Discharging a firearm at another is always considered the use of deadly force, regardless of the outcome. For someone to be justified in the use of deadly force, the surviving victim must have reasonably believed the use of deadly force was necessary while acting in self-defense to prevent an attack that would result in serious bodily injury or death. This bodily injury must be imminent in the mind of a reasonable person.

The problem with a trap gun is the lack of a reasonable person behind the trigger since the firearm's discharge is automatic."[59]

Escaping

There are situations where you may have to go ahead and abandon your fortress home, no matter how distasteful this may prove to be. The forces may prove to be superior to your ability to defend against them. Your home may get set on fire past your ability to extinguish those fires. Though you want to stay put and lay low as much as possible during an emergency, you can't guarantee that you won't have to leave. It shouldn't be your first choice—it should be a last resort, especially if you've taken the time to fortify your home to the degree that we're preparing you to do in this book. That said, there could be times when an escape might mean your life.

Once you've escaped the home, however, you're just at the beginning of your problems. You'll be moving through what amounts to hostile enemy territory if the rioting and looting are widespread. This is also the case if you are nowhere near your home when rioting and looting break out. In that scenario, you'd need to carefully make your way back to your home so that you can hunker down, lay low, and defend it if necessary. In either case your situation is much more dangerous because you will be on the move.

It's a good idea to scout your city and create a series of pre-arranged "PACE" routes for the places you go the most (work, your child's daycare, the grocery store, etc.) PACE stands for "Primary, Alternative, Contingency, and Emergency." That means you're literally going to think of four different ways to get to where you need to go.[60]

You also need a place to run *to* if your own home is overrun. This could be the home of a family member or trusted friend, your church, or anywhere else where you think you could be safe. Becoming a wandering refugee during the worst of times is a sketchy proposition at best—you need to be able to make your way with purpose. In some scenarios you might only need to make it out of town and to a place where you might be able to make your way to a hotel, but be aware that in emergencies such things are hard to come by for miles around. During evacuations for Hurricane Katrina, it was nearly impossible to find a single hotel or a good traffic-free route as far north as the Arkansas border. You also might well be in a situation where you can't get to your vehicle or can't fuel it sufficiently. If this happens you might have to make part of your escape on foot. You may have to make these decisions in a split second, so preparing contingency plans for several different scenarios before problems arise is your best bet. It's also possible that there *will* be nowhere viable for you to go, in which case you need to have pre-identified an area where you can go and attempt to live off the land until better options arise.

Once you've decided to escape, you're going to need some sort of initial regrouping location if your final destination isn't close enough for you to reach. This is a place where you can be somewhat safe long enough to get some first aid, to take some inventory, and to check your routes so you can go over your maps one more time and make sure you know what you're doing.[61]

Once you start moving, you're going to be vulnerable to all kinds of attacks. You might need to move, stop, hide, assess, and then move again. Though you're not exactly dealing with a military scenario, you should treat your immediate area as "enemy territory," since enemies drove you out of your home in the first place.

"It is usually better to move at night because of the concealment that darkness offers. Exceptions to such movements would be

while moving through hazardous terrain or dense vegetation.

Movement in enemy-held terrain is a very slow and deliberate process. The slower you move and the more careful you are, the better. Your best security will be using your senses. Use your eyes and ears to detect people before they detect you. Make frequent listening halts. In daylight, observe a section of your route before you move along it. The distance you travel before you hide will depend on the enemy situation, your health, the terrain, the availability of cover and concealment for hiding, and the amount of darkness left."[62]

Again, this is a worst-case scenario. If at all possible, you want to stay in your fortified location with all of your supplies readily to hand. This is also the best case for your long-term mental health. Don't leave unless you absolutely have to. In Chapter 8 we'll cover more thoughts on bugging out versus staying in place, and how these decisions relate to your overall security strategy.

Stocking Up Safely

Your chances of having to deal with looters go up exponentially if people know for a fact that you already have a good stockpile of emergency supplies. This also increases your chances of having to deal with hungry, desperate people who wouldn't think of stealing from you, but who will knock on your door and beg. Deciding whether to give up precious supplies to a hungry mother or whether to send that mother on her way with her starving children will be an individual decision, something you'll have to prayerfully make when the time comes. However, too many such benign visitors could wind up being just as dangerous as the looters. You could whittle away your supplies until you have very little to protect. It's best to deal with as few strangers as possible, no matter what methods they employ to try to get their hands on your supplies.

Observing certain safety precautions as you're actively building your stashes and stockpiles could be one of the most important security measures you ever take. This doesn't mean that you're toting a gun as you make your way back from the grocery store with your latest three-month supply of food. On the contrary, it means that you will need to lay low and blend in wherever possible. This will be important whether you're defending against looters or worrying about martial law or confiscation scenarios.

Think of it this way. If you scatter trash all over your yard and your neighbors aren't sure you had anything anyway, they'll probably be more likely to quickly move on. But if you scatter trash all over your yard and everyone on your block knows that you've stashed a year's worth of food and water somewhere in your home, they might want to attack anyway... just to "double check."

Prepare Gradually

Having a year's supply of food shipped to your home or unloading a truck full of box after box of canned goods is a sure way to get attention from your neighbors. Today, they may just think you're an eccentric. Tomorrow, when problems arise, they might remember those big boxes of food making their way into your home.

Or, picture a scenario where you've got government officials intent on taking stockpiles of supplies from private citizens under "hoarding" laws, intent on "redistributing them" so that everyone can be in poverty and misery together. Purchase records from your credit cards make it clear what you've bought—but if you've built up your stockpile by buying three or four extra items every time you go to the store it's likely they'll assume that those groceries were consumed with the rest of your groceries during each shopping period rather than assuming you're hiding those groceries somewhere in your home. Since manpower and time will still be issues for any martial-law scenario, thugs are more likely to target homes which they *know* have extra food and water than homes which seem like every other home on the block.

Using this method also saves your pocketbook. It's not wise to go into debt to buy a bunch of bulk supplies or specialty supplies, especially if you're buying cases of food you've never eaten or tried because it's being marketed as a special "survival" food. Instead, buy extras of items that you use on a regular basis, take advantage of coupons and "buy one get one free" specials. Rotate out your stockpile on a regular basis, and you'll find it easy, natural, and most importantly, low-key.

Prepare Secretly

While you don't have to go crazy with secrecy to the point where you attract attention by appearing paranoid and weird, it is a good idea to treat your stockpiles as being "need-to-know" information—don't tell anybody who doesn't need to know.

> *"Silence means security...Loose talk is a direct delivery to the enemy. If you want to swagger around, bragging about your 'preparations' then by all means do so, but with the understanding that you may as well have just laid your [supplies] out on the front lawn and invited law enforcement or the thugs down the street to come get them."*[63]

You might even want to be careful about any participation in forums or survival groups. You're broadcasting your identity, and not everyone you are talking to will be trustworthy. The very enemies you are trying to defend against may be monitoring these groups for the express purpose of knowing who is doing what.

In addition, you might consider using cash to pay for many of your supplies. This can conceal the true extent of the supplies that you are buying from folks who might have the ability to dig into your credit card statements or personal affairs.

Once you get your items home, you'll want to make sure you keep them out of plain view. You don't want to flaunt your gear, no matter what it is. If you have something that you have to leave in plain sight, have explanations ready. If you have a fancy water purifier, for example, you can tell visitors that it just, "Makes the water taste better." The more you can keep out of sight, the better!

You should be careful about who you invite into your home anyway. Most burglaries are perpetrated by people who have been inside of the home. This gives them ample time to check out the valuables, look at the layout of your home, and figure out how to get away with their crime. Keep the visitors down to a minimum. Sure, the odd babysitter or repairman is unavoidable. Of course, you want to be able to have your friends over for coffee. But don't be indiscriminate, and don't leave people in your home unattended. You never know when you might be setting yourself up for an inside job later down the line or a scenario where your repair guy tells his buddies, "I know where we can score a whole bunch of food."

Safety While Transporting Valuables

Gold, silver, firearms: These are three items that are always valuable and that are always likely to draw some level of attention. There are risks to buying these items online, and there are risks to buying them in person too. Online, there is little hope that you'll be able to conceal the fact that you have made the purchase. In person you need to be alert to the possibility that someone is going to attempt to follow you home and steal what you have just bought.

When you're driving home after making one of these purchases, check your rearview mirror frequently to see if you can spot a follower. If you think you're being followed, you can take three consecutive right hand turns or three consecutive left hand turns. If you still see a follower it's time to drive somewhere safe instead of driving home, perhaps even to your local police station.[64]

At some future date if you find yourself using your gold or silver to buy food for you and your family, carry only a little at a time and stay on high alert. Be sure that nobody is able to follow you back to your home, and be careful with whom you trade. It would be best if your trading partners don't know your end-location so they can't pass on the information to a large group of people who might come after your gold and silver later!

Blending In and Advanced Hiding Techniques

Keeping a low profile is going to be your best bet in any scenario where you are in danger of having to use or defend your stockpiles. It's important that you look as much like everyone else as possible. You don't want to have the home that outwardly looks more prosperous than every other home on the block. You don't want to walk outside in nearly new clothes if everyone around you is in tattered rags. Blending in with your neighbors is just a good security procedure for today or tomorrow, no matter what the circumstances.

In fact, if you're growing any kind of survival garden on your property, you might want to consider doing so in a stealthy manner so that the garden itself isn't targeted in the event of an attack by looters! Having a survival garden, particularly a large survival garden, is at least a signal to the looters that they should come pick your harvest clean. It's better if you can make sure they can't find it.

There are a lot of creative ways to hide a survival garden. For example, you could try secret grow rooms.

"Secret grow rooms or green houses should be considered. All that is needed in most cases is to remove the roof for a garage

or outbuilding and replace it with corrugated fiberglass. The walls can be painted white or covered with aluminum foil to help reflect light back on the plants inside. From the outside it looks like any other building while inside grows an abundant garden."[65]

Another method you might consider trying is simply to use plants that blend in well with other, less edible plants.

"Some plants are easier to hide than others; potatoes, for instance, would be easier to hide than say, tomatoes. Most people would pass within three feet of a stand of potatoes and not recognize what they were looking at. Choosing plants that blend in with the surroundings is an important consideration for the survival gardener."[66]

If you're interested in other stealth survival garden methods, you might consider picking up a copy of *Rising Prices, Empty Shelves* from Solutions from Science. The book will also give you several indicators that can tell you when all of these Phase 3 security measures may become more important than ever.

You should also consider creating some hiding spaces for your precious metals, food supplies, and other valuables similar to the hiding spaces that you created for your guns. In fact, these sorts of hiding places could get even more elaborate, allowing you to create much larger stockpiles inside of your home. This could even mean creating a small, secret room or space.

Creating a secret room or space will be out of reach for most renters and apartment dwellers, but it's remarkably simple if you're a homeowner. If you have a closet that isn't obvious (like a hall closet—don't use as bedroom closet as it would be more noticeable that it was "missing"), you can conceal it with a bookshelf that could be pushed aside in the event that you need to get to your stash. Or you could get an actual bookshelf door from www.spacexdoors.com. If you have a large walk-in closet, you can shrink it and add a secret door that appears to be a simple full-length mirror; they sell them at www.hiddenpassageway.com. You might even be able to create something similar by adding a false wall with a crawlspace and then hanging a mirror in front of it. In the event that your home does get looted (perhaps while you are away) or robbed, you may at least be able to use the supplies that were hidden away and unlikely to be detected in such an out of the way spot. In this case you're not looking for a full room, as you would have been for the safe room, but just a small spot to stack additional supplies so that you're not left with nothing if you happen to be away when looting breaks out or if you have to flee. If you do have to flee, you could potentially come back and re-inhabit your home once the danger has passed, and in this fashion you avoid losing your shelter as well as some of your supplies.

CHAPTER 7

ෆ•ෆ

TRAINING THE FAMILY ON PERSONAL SELF-DEFENSE AND FIRST AID

Training the Family on Personal Self-Defense and First Aid

ဢ • ൙

Much has been said on survival forums and blogs on the importance of carefully and quietly linking up with like-minded people in the event of a disaster. Whether you're looking at a Rawlesian retreat or an Evensen model of community leadership, there's no denying that you're going to *need* other people to survive whatever comes your way. That's why this manual has already stressed connecting with your community in a natural way. Nobody can do it all, and you'll spread yourself pretty thin pretty quickly if you try.

However, in the rush to prepare, it can be easy to overlook the place where you're most likely to find reliable, trustworthy help. The family. The family will be the people you can count on, the ones you'll need to fall back on. If your home is attacked and there's nobody around for miles, it will be up to the family to defend that home or to come up with some sort of cohesive plan for escaping it. Figuring out where all of your family members are and regrouping in the event of a disaster could wind up being priority number one if you're not conveniently located at your home at the time when things fall apart. Some disasters come with plenty of warning. Others happen in a heartbeat—while Dad's at work, Mom is at the supermarket (or more commonly these days, also at work), Junior is at a basketball game, and Sister is at ballet.

Getting Your Family On Board

Your family might not bat an eyelash when you get a security system installed and plant a cactus beneath every window. But they might start exhibiting a very different reaction when you start talking about safe rooms, guns, and training the family on what to do in the event of a crisis. Everybody is not always happy to talk about preparing for a dark and uncertain future. Since good preparation takes both time and money— time to learn the skills and money to acquire the equipment you will need to defend your home—you might find yourself in some protracted battles with an unwilling spouse over the survival mindset. Those of you lucky enough to have a spouse who is open to the possibilities inherent in the need to prepare might still be dealing with children who aren't so interested in preparing for the various scenarios.

How well you overcome this initial hurdle will be one of the major factors in whether or not your family survives an economic collapse, an attack by looters, or even just a simple increase in crime. A family that isn't fully invested may humor you, but they won't take it seriously and so less of it will "stick."

Primarily, you want to make sure you're not forcing the topic on your family. Going on long rants about the problems you see on the horizon is a guaranteed way to make your family members tune out. Nobody likes having ideas shoved down their throat, and for some reason many people have a switch in their heads which makes them overload with panic if they have to contemplate the idea that life won't always turn out as well as they'd planned or hoped. Unloading the wors- case scenarios on your family all at once will cause them to react in mental self-defense—by flinging themselves even harder into this present reality, where things are still going relatively well and safely. Instead, you need to be initiating discussions. Use events in the news, books, television shows, and movies to start "what if" discussions. What if someone broke into our home? What if we were in the path of that hurricane? What if we had an economic collapse like Argentina did?

As your family comes up with suggestions on what they think they would do, listen. Encourage them. If some of the ideas are bad, don't say so outright. Just say, "That's a good idea; how could we make it better?" If you can get your family members thinking and interested on their own, you can eventually lead them to a place where they *want* to get prepared.[67]

If this still doesn't work, you can simply continue to take steps while exposing any interested family member into any aspect of preparedness that you can. Your sixteen-year-old daughter wants to babysit? Make her take first aid courses first. Take your son camping and teach him how to shoot. Your wife gripes about the cost of food? Mention that it's only going up and suggest she buy one or two extras every time she goes to the store. Once things start going wrong, your influence will still rub off on them enough that you'll still be better off than families that couldn't pull together at all.

Planning and Practice

Everybody in your family is different. They have different ages and different capacities for dealing with stress. The surest way to make sure that everybody is able to survive in spite of their differences is to make sure that some things aren't that new to them. That means having plans in place right now, before things go wrong.

One way to do this is to develop a survival handbook for your home and family. This was the suggestion of the Suburban Survival Blog, who brought to mind similar handbooks that you might actually find at your workplace or school.

"Every home should have a Home Crisis Handbook....It is a small book that you can build that will have tabs and/or pages dedicated to different disasters such as earthquake, tornado, hurricane, fire in the home, home invasion, etc... each page should have a color-coded tab so it is easy to find the... situation and each page should have explicit instructions on

how to handle the [situation] in a moment of panic. This will give you a preparedness plan for each situation you could possibly encounter, and it will give each individual, without fail, instructions on what to do, where to go, and how to get out of a situation that is potentially deadly."[68]

Even if your family can't access the book in the event of a crisis, they will remember the book, and perhaps remember the family planning sessions that put it together. This can give you a bank of standard operating procedures so that you don't have to reinvent the wheel every time something new comes up.

If your family is 100% on board, you can run drills or rehearsals for home invasions, attacks by looters, or any number of other scenarios. These can be verbal rehearsals, or they can be actual physical rehearsals where younger children get to the safe room and the adults and older children man the window weapons. Each time you rehearse, you reduce the chances that someone will endanger the family by freezing up or panicking at a crucial moment.

Setting a Watch

Sleep is a survival necessity. Inadequate sleep robs a person of their ability to perform and can lead to hallucinations and severe mental distress. That's why sleep deprivation is actually a form of torture! In some scenarios everything you've done to turn your home into a fortress will be more than enough to make it safe for you and your family to sleep through the night as normal.

In other scenarios you're going to want someone to stay awake in order to keep watch. That means you're going to have to set up a rotating sleep schedule. You're going to have to make sure that each member of the family is calm enough not to jump at shadows or to enact security protocols without need, but is also alert enough to make sure that they pay attention. This is where your surveillance devices can come in handy—someone watching cameras is going to be far less jumpy than someone peering out into the darkness, wondering what every noise and shadow could be.

Try to come up with a watch schedule as part of your protocols right now, so that everyone will be able to run the watch smoothly. Practice your watch protocols while there isn't anything wrong so that everyone will be better equipped to handle the watch should the need ever arise. This can also help you decide which members of your family are old enough to stay awake during their shift and which members are likely to fall asleep or grow inattentive.

Finding One Another

Your family plans should include scenarios where something goes horribly wrong and someone is separated from the house. This includes thinking about communications protocols as well as meeting places. These plans could be simple matters of drawing out PACE routes for each of your family's most common destinations and then stating: If there is a disaster, drop what you are doing and try to get home. If you can't get home or you're in a state of lock down, try to send a text message every half hour till you get through to someone. If home is not an option because there's a state- or city-wide evacuation going on, we will all continue to try to travel until we get to grandmother's house one state away (or wherever). Again, much will depend on the composition of your family and community— you might tell younger children to get to the nearest school or church and stay there until a parent or older child arrives to pick them up rather than sending them through a PACE route to walk seven miles across town to the house by themselves. Use your common sense and think through contingencies that are applicable to your area.

Text messages and e-mails get through the network more reliably in a crisis than phone calls do. Each family member should also be required to know or carry vital phone numbers for the house itself and for other family members so they can get in touch with them in the event of a crisis. Too many of us keep our lives inside of our cell phone; if the battery dies or the cell phone is lost, that precludes being able to get to another phone and make a call.

It would also be a good idea for families to be up to date on each member's routine and for it to be a requirement for each family member to let the others know where they will be in the event of a crisis.

Ask a family member who doesn't live in the area if they'll be willing to be the authorized point of contact in the event that something goes wrong. If you can find something like this, the family can focus on getting their status and location to this one person who can pass on the information to all the others, rather than trying to keep in touch with one another locally, where getting through might be much harder.

Turning the Family into a Unit

Assuming that everyone will at some point make it home, and assuming that you will have to "dig in" to protect your home from looters and thugs, it would be wise to treat your family as its own sort of military unit. That's not to say that you want to turn your home into the Army or anything, with the family leader barking orders and the children doing push-ups. It's just that everyone needs to be trained on one primary job and cross-trained on a secondary job, so that everyone knows how to contribute. The smallest of children, of course, will be exempt from this. However, even a four year old can be trained so that "feeding and changing the baby" is their primary job, freeing up Mom to do something else. This will make it far easier to pull together in the event of a protracted crisis. Of course, there will always be general chores that will have to be done, and those can be assigned at need.

This is one of those situations where you can turn the diversity of your family to your advantage. When people first get started with preparations, they tend to gravitate towards the area that they're most comfortable with. The person in your family who already likes to hunt and fish might get heavily focused on guns and self-defense, for example. The one who likes to cook might get more fixated on gardening and food storage. The one who enjoys being on the Internet all day long might get focused on radios and communications. Since any number of survival tasks will be extremely useful, encourage the interest. If your son feels that cell phones won't be enough and wants to set up a centralized radio network in your home and be in charge of manning the communication station in a crisis—then let him do it. Practice it with him. Talk about how he will handle it if he's not there in the event something goes wrong—will he write down each message on a portable notebook and relay information that way? Another family member may like picking up wounded birds and bringing them home to tend. That family member might be a prime candidate to receive advanced first aid training. If you let each family member expand on their own interest and then cross-train anyone who is old enough on the use of a weapon, basic first aid, and home defense protocols, then you'll have a tight knit, very useful family who is able to pull together in a crisis.

The Presence of Kids Requires Special Survival Supplies and Skills

Imagine for a moment that the worst has happened, and you have to escape from your home. Have you given any thought to the special tools that having children will virtually require you to have?

You won't want to try escaping your home by putting an infant into a stroller or a car seat, for example. After a mile of trying to lug the baby around that way someone's back and arms are going to be very tired.

Yet simply holding the baby means someone's hands aren't free to wield a weapon, manage a radio, or help out with simple tasks. That means you're going to want a baby sling that allows someone to hold the baby close to their body while keeping their arms free. It also means you might want to consider abandoning formula as an option as each baby is born and sticking to breast feeding (if medically possible—not all women can breast feed). This makes the baby's food far more portable and means that the baby doesn't have to depend so much on iffy water supplies. If you have babies, you're also going to need cloth diapers, diaper pins, diaper pails, and bleach—if things are so bad that you're having to worry about defending your home from looters, chances are high that you're not going to be able to get out to buy disposable diapers when you need them. Stocking up on enough disposable diapers to handle every stage of a baby's growth during a crisis amounts to a form of madness—think about how many diapers the average baby goes through in a single day, factor in the different sizes you'll likely need, and you'll soon realize you'd need an entire room of your house devoted to nothing but disposable diapers if you wanted to make those part of your preparations.[69]

If you have a family, you also need an emergency back-up shelter for the whole family. If you bought a "pre-generated" bug-out bag at any point, you might have noticed that it came with a simple "tube tent"—but how many people will that sleep? You'll also need kid-friendly multi-vitamins for the older children, just in case they get picky about what they eat in a survival situation. And they might—stress will make children want to revert back to the familiar and safe.[70]

You'll also need some specific parenting skills to help you see your children through a change in their world big enough to require this level of preparation. Disasters affect kids in very specific ways, and they might start acting up or acting out in a way that's not terribly conducive to security if you can't help them out.

"Preparing for a disaster and coping with it afterwards can sometimes be difficult for children and their families. Children may be frightened by the disaster itself, or be upset by disruptions that a disaster may cause in their daily routines or their relationships with parents, teachers, and friends. It is not unusual for children to show changes in behavior that may be signs or symptoms of distress or discomfort following a disaster."[71]

It's going to be important for you to keep children informed without sugar coating what's going on, using simple language. But you also need to take the time to reassure them that you've done everything possible to keep them safe. Remind them of all the preparations you've made. Take the time to give them hugs and kisses and remind them that you're going to come through this together, as a family. Continue to suggest ways that they can help so they don't feel helpless, overwhelmed, and small as their worlds get upside down.[72]

CHAPTER 8

ഇ•ര

MARTIAL LAW —WHEN YOU ARE THE CRIMINAL

Martial Law—
When YOU are the Criminal

ඝා•ൟ

If you are reading this book there's a good chance that someone thinks you're a terrorist.

Bold words.

Sadly, they are words based in fact. We can say them with a certainty because the government has released publication after publication that makes *almost everyone* a terrorist.

The FBI's Joint Terrorism Task Force pamphlet says you're a terrorist if you're willing to defend the U.S. Constitution against the federal government and the U.N. If you've ever taken any training that someone could label as "para-military" training, you're also on the list (be aware that the FBI even monitors historical reenactment groups that practice mock warfare as a form of "para-military training"). If you have ever made numerous references to the U.S. Constitution, stood up against abortion, believe in animal rights, or are any kind of environmentalist...you just might be a terrorist.[73]

Or how about the Missouri Information Analysis Center (MIAC), which issued a report on domestic terrorism? This report says you're a potential terrorist if you've ever opposed the New World Order (or even talked about it), spoken out against the United Nations, supported gun control, complained about violations of *posse comitatus*, opposed fiat currency and the manipulations of the Federal Reserve, supported a new Constitutional Convention, spoken out against a North American Union, opposed a universal service program, shown concern over RFID chips, or spoken out about the NAFTA super highway. To this extensive list you can also add anyone who opposes abortions on demand, is against illegal immigration, or supported certain political candidates (namely Ron Paul, Chuck Baldwin, or Bob Barr).[74]

If you still don't fit into any of these categories, rest assured that our highly frightened and paranoid government is still naming terrorists based on their race or religion, just as they did during World War II to American citizens of Japanese descent. Arab Americans still have plenty of cause for concern, as do blacks. Practicing Muslims have already been singled out. For example, former CIA director R. James Woolsey and former Deputy Undersecretary of Defense for Intelligence Lt. Gen. William G. Boyken published a book called *Shariah: The Threat to America,* in which they alleged that "nearly every" mosque in the United States has already been "radicalized" and that "most" Muslim social organizations are fronts for violent jihadists. 75 This is not good news if you happen to be, say, an American Muslim who just wants to gather with other Muslim students over coffee on a college campus. There are terrorist threats, and some of them do come from violent extremists among Muslims, among racist hate groups, among all sorts of quarters. But profiling an entire group or religion as being "potential terrorists" before they've done anything wrong is a violation of the First Amendment and a violation of the spirit of religious freedom which founded this country in the first place.

Yes, Christians need to be concerned—that gun could easily be trained on Christians as a whole.

•

The point of all this information is, in truth, that almost *any justification* is now being used to slap a "terrorist" label on people that the government finds scary, inconvenient, threatening, or unlikely to quietly submit to the agenda. If you don't find yourself *anywhere* on the above lists, don't assume that you're safe. These lists often include references to "subversive literature" too. It's not hard to name any book or film as "subversive." This book advocates having guns and hiding them around the house—is it coming to a subversive literature list near you?

The amount of surveillance that ordinary citizens are already under is staggering and frightening.

"...The United States is assembling a vast domestic intelligence apparatus to collect information about Americans, using the FBI, local police, state homeland security offices and military criminal investigations. This system, by far the largest and most technologically sophisticated in the nation's history, collects, stores, and analyzes information about thousands of U.S. citizens and residents, many of whom have not been accused of any wrong doing.

The FBI is building a database with the names and certain personal information such as employment history of thousands of U.S. citizens and residents whom local police officers or a fellow citizen believed to be acting suspiciously."[76]

It is not at all unreasonable to assume that a day could come where *you* are considered the criminal. This is the opposite end of the disaster spectrum. On one hand you have anarchy, looting, rioting, and dangerous shoot-outs outside of your own door.

On the other, you have to fear those who are supposed to be protecting you. This is the Phase 4 scenario.

What is Life Like Under Martial Law?

It is very difficult for the average American to really conceive of what nation-wide martial law would look like. Many of us are still hard-wired to think of authority figures as "the good guys." That means it is useful to gather some pictures of what martial law has looked like in other countries. Remember that under a long-term martial-law scenario the

Constitution will be completely disregarded. A military commander will be in charge, and everything will be running under military rules.

Here's one voice from the Philippines.

"It was a very awful time to live in the Philippines during Martial Law. This horrid law was ruled by President Marcos. I believe it was declared in September 1971, though I do not remember the actual date. It became listed in 1983 though. The people of the Philippines wanted to rebel this law ever since it was determined by President Marcos. No one agreed to this law, and it caused much destruction amongst the whole country.

One of the things I can remember from Martial Law was the curfew that was set up. It was around eleven o'clock, that if you were still on the road, the...police would cite you for that... the police did not treat people in a...well, nice way.

There weren't ways that a justice system could help the people because there wasn't one at that time! Can you imagine how much more oppressive it was to live in a country without a justice system? This became a reason why Marcos and his men were able to do many villainous things.

There were many times when Marcos and his men would even kidnap people who were after the government. These men were feared by many."[77]

A 2003 BBC News report also gives some poignant images from martial law in the Aceh region of Indonesia. Reporter Rachel Harvey interviewed Dewi, a twenty-year-old biology student, and Arif, a twenty-one-year-old engineering student.

"Arif said people in Aceh were beginning to get used to life under martial law, but still tended to panic when they heard gunfire.

'The problem is the military doesn't always seem to be able to tell the difference between civilians and rebels,' he said.

'On the second day of the Idul Fitri holiday, two people were shot dead in the middle of Banda Aceh. I don't know if they were rebels or not, but they certainly weren't military.'

[Dewi]…said few people in her village were working normally.

Farmers check to see whether there are any soldiers about before they risk going to tend their paddy fields.

'The problem is the military are suspicious that local farmers might be giving food to the rebels. Sometimes they get beaten up, or just disappear.'

Dewi said a culture of fear and suspicion permeated everything."[78]

Curfews. Confiscation of arms, equipment, and sometimes even food. Neighbors turning in neighbors due to old grudges, or just to get in favor with the occupying forces so they can feather their own nests. Ordinary citizens becoming the targets of violence, imprisonment, and smear campaigns. Restrictions on citizen movement, checkpoints, and the need for elaborate papers. Corruption, bribery, and fear. People getting dragged off to detention centers in the night, never to be seen again. All of this is nothing more than the documented affects of martial law, from Aceh to Nazi Germany.

Such a situation may be so terrifying to contemplate that it's difficult to even imagine defending your home, your family, or your person under such circumstances. However, there are things you can do.

Avoiding Notice

In a martial-law situation your primary priority is going to be to avoid as much notice as possible. Keep your head down and go quietly about your business as much as possible. Otherwise you risk becoming a target for the occupying force to make an example of. You should also use the caching strategies later in this chapter to make sure some of your guns are far away from your property. That means you can peacefully turn over whatever you have in your house in the event of a door-to-door search without losing access to all weapons.[79] Be careful about hiding guns around your home. If you've taken the time to cache, you might just want to dig out these hidden weapons and turn them over with the rest. Finding *deliberately hidden weapons* in your home might well inspire the troops to arrest you on the spot. They won't assume they're there to defend you against criminals and robbers—they'll assume you have them to resist the troops. They also might not particularly *care* why you have them, and they certainly won't care about your need to defend yourself. Our government already demonstrated this in New Orleans during the gun confiscation fiasco that it enacted during Hurricane Katrina.

If everyone else is suffering without inadequate access to food and water, be sure to pace your own eating habits. You don't want to look like you're living well and staying healthy while everyone else is in trouble.[80] Stay quiet—don't give any information to anyone. You never know who might turn you in for their own reasons! Remember, loose lips sink ships.

Avoid trying to go anywhere you do not absolutely have to go. If you have to go to work, go to work and go home. Don't make any unnecessary trips. Avoid government checkpoints whenever and wherever possible. Don't challenge any military officials, and stay as polite and as harmless as you possibly can.

Caching

Being declared a criminal might mean that you lose access to food and weapons. It might well mean that you will find yourself on the run sometime in the future, even if you've done nothing wrong. This means you are going to need to have put some things away in advance in order to be prepared for this sort of dark day. The best way to go about this is caching—hiding the things you'll need far away from your property and secretly so that you may one day retrieve them and use them.

First, you will need to identify out-of-the way places where you can do some digging in peace. These spots need to have some good identifying landmarks. It also helps if you have a GPS system that you can use to locate the cache in the future. You should also take pictures of the area before you start digging, as you will want to restore it to its previous state. Otherwise someone can find your cache simply because you didn't do a good enough job of hiding that something of interest has gone on at the site. You can also cache in urban locations, such as in dark, abandoned buildings. Remove a few bricks from the wall and then replace them to create an improvised vault. It's best to have several caches spread out over multiple locations.[81]

In terms of a martial-law situation one particular cache that you'll want to make sure you have on hand is an "Escape and Evasion" cache:

"The E&E cache (Escape and Evasion) will have a complete getaway kit in addition to a pistol or folding-stock rifle and ammunition. The E&E cache is meant to be well-hidden but able to be grabbed up at a moment's notice. You'll have stuff to treat injuries in this cache, as well as items to use to change your appearance such as scissors and hair dye, water purification tablets, and MREs. Including several hundred dollars worth of cash in here would be prudent—in ten- and twenty-dollar denominations."[82]

Of course, you will need somewhere to go and hide, but where you go in this scenario will depend on the circumstances. Some small towns may not be so locked down, or you might have to make the decision to hide in the wilderness for a time. At a time like this, you will have to stay alert and stay intelligent to stay free.

Escape Routes

The same exercises on escape routes and potential alternative locations that you performed during your Phase 3 looting scenarios will come in handy if you have to slip away in the event of a martial-law scenario. You should have routes from your home, from work, and anywhere you go regularly, and you should identify potential places that you can go to escape detection later. You need to take steps to be familiar with your area because you don't want to be running blind if there's a hunt on for you or people like you. In this case, though, you need to make sure you're avoiding high traffic areas. You want trails off the beaten path, not major streets.

However, if all goes well you shouldn't have to resort to such extreme measures. Your well-stocked, low-key fortress home should allow you to stay off the streets and out of the public eye of any sort of martial-law scenario. Not all martial-law scenarios involve house-to-house searches, and if this is the case you should be able to steer clear of trouble by staying put as much as possible and as long as possible. Eventually the martial-law situation will calm down a bit, and you should be able to survive by staying out of sight and blending in.

$\wp \bullet \wp$

CHAPTER 9

 મ • ન

BUGGING OUT VS. STAYING IN PLACE

Bugging Out vs. Staying in Place

ℰ •ℛ

Most of the time when people write about a major crisis the emphasis is on "bugging out"—a sort of "best case" evacuation strategy where you take a backpack full of necessities and escape whatever danger is threatening. However, this book has taught you more about how to fortify your current position so that you can stay put! It's worth examining when bugging out is a good idea, when it isn't, and where you can best position yourself *before* you start making all the investments and improvements that a fully fortified home will demand.

The Backpacker and the "Retreat"

Those who favor bugging out no matter what tend to come in one of two camps. One camp favors the "retreat" strategy, where a family or a group of families go buy a big property in the middle of nowhere and try to man it with military precision 24/7 while simultaneously farming it and living off of the land.

The second camp involves people who have a vision of escaping danger—especially danger that comes from an oppressive society—by slipping off into the woods, hiding out there in a tent, teepee, dug-out home, or woodsman survival shelter long term—and living off the land using their wits, their skills, and the contents of their seventy-two-hour bug-out bag.

There are real issues with either strategy. The retreat strategy, first of all, is a strategy that depends on you remaining unfound at least one tank of gas away from any major city. Before any crisis hits, this means being far away from most of the jobs that are out there. If you don't plan on living at your retreat, you'll wind up having to pay a second mortgage to see to its upkeep. You also have to find people who want to come out there and live at your retreat with you, either right now or when the time comes, because you won't be able to defend it alone.

> *"There is strength in numbers. Rugged individualism is all well and good, but it takes more than one man to defend a retreat. Effective retreat defense necessitates having at least two families to provide 24/7 perimeter security. But of course every individual added means another mouth to feed. Absent having an unlimited budget and an infinite larder, this necessitates striking a balance when deciding the size of a retreat group."*[83]

Assuming you've found two to four families who are willing to share your retreat and who get along with you well enough to give the basic skeleton security, that might give your retreat some hope of safety. You can't count on not being found, as almost any location in the United States can be found by *someone*. The question is whether or not your group of families can ever possibly be enough versus dedicated criminals or looters who will stake out your location. In remote rural locations, no help is on the way, and you might become an even more desirable target than your counterparts in major cities or small towns. A crime nightmare scenario such as the ones we've discussed in this book make the retreat philosophy an increasingly risky proposition.

> *"I don't think an isolated homestead or farm is the best place to be in, and it certainly isn't when crime becomes a real problem all across the country. Unless you have dedicated security, all day long, all year long, it's impossible to defend such a place.*

Your isolation and lack of neighbors means criminals can be more bold, spend more time during the invasions without fear of being detected...the homestead will also have more appealing loot than an average downtown or suburban home, and the risk of getting caught while perpetrating the crime is also less."[84]

Mel Tappan was easily one of the fathers of the modern preparedness movement. In his 1981 book *Tappan on Survival*, he pointed out some very real problems with the idea of an isolated hideaway:

"Once you have reached the point where you feel that preparedness is no longer academic, and you have a growing, apprehensive awareness that the time grows short for you to relocate away from the areas of greatest danger, it becomes increasingly easy to see the shortcomings of the traditional retreat alternatives. The seagoing approach, for example, is simply out of the question for more than a miniscule few; the land mobile techniques so widely touted by at least one writer are patently irresponsible; isolated wilderness retreats are virtually indefensible by the average family; group retreats sound good in theory but once you begin investigating actual examples, serious problems become apparent."[85]

Unless you are going to live at your retreat full time, you have the issue of whether or not you're going to even be able to make it there once trouble starts. Everyone will find out about the disaster at roughly the same time. Traffic congestion becomes a real problem. During Hurricane Rita, millions of cars turned every one of Houston's major interstates into a parking lot. State highways, farm routes, and other parts of the "less beaten path" were no better—unless you were headed back *in* to the city. Taking a southbound route through Houston by 11 p.m. on Wednesday, September 21, 2005, as the then-category five hurricane seemed to all but swallow the

Gulf of Mexico was an eerie sight indeed. One or two cars were speeding back home, perhaps from work or other obligations, as the northbound routes became hopeless snarls from the downtown loop forward.

Those who braved the traffic soon found out how quickly a city runs out of supplies. By 3 a.m. stores and fast food restaurants were putting up stark, simple, horrifying signs which read: NO FOOD. Gas stations were having to put up similar signs that read: NO GAS. One was lucky to make it out of the city five or six hours later. Evacuation routes came under the control of law enforcement. After awhile they told drivers where to go—it was possible to be a driver trying to find your way to higher ground while having absolutely no idea where you were. Many cars wound up stranded, uselessly, on the side of the road as they ran out of gas. People died in the evacuation process alone. If you were lucky enough to have a low-gas mileage car, wise enough not to run the air conditioner, and took just the right routes, some twelve hours later you would have been able to find the gas station far enough away from Houston to have some gas—and to be willing to sell you just ten dollars of that gas before forcing you to move on. This is what *any* major urban evacuation would look like, and "retreat-level catastrophes," where societal order has broken down completely, would look even worse.

Assuming you do get to your retreat you also have to face the possibility that someone might be squatting there by the time you get there. If you fortified your retreat to the degree that we've advocated fortifying your primary home you are then in the position of having to somehow root out the squatters. If you're very lucky they'll leave voluntarily. If you're somewhat lucky you might be able to negotiate their presence as one of the families that will help you defend the home, and negotiate your place in your own property. From then on you would have to trust your own family's safety to an uncertain and untrustworthy lot.

Of course, you could always try to leave early and live in your retreat right now, but can you afford to?

"This is one of the ugly realities of our situation today--most families won't leave urban areas in time because they can't afford leaving early and being wrong. Why? Because it means abandoning your house, friends, job, sometimes even family. If you leave and are too early can you get your job back? Be thankful you didn't bug out in April 2009 for the flu "pandemic." If you leave too early and can't pay your mortgage, will the bank understand?"[86]

What about the backpacker, who intends to live off the land wherever and however he can? What kind of challenge will this person face as he or she "bugs out?" A 1989 article in the *American Survival Guide* by Duncan Long provides a rather succinct answer:

"A 'backpack survivalist' is a survivalist that plans on leaving his home ahead of a disaster and taking to the woods with only what he can carry out with him. He plans to survive through a strategy that is sort of a cross between Boy-Scout-in-the-Woods and Robinson Crusoe. The backpack survivalist plans on outrunning danger with a four-wheel drive or a motorcycle and hopes to travel light with a survival kit of everything he might need to cope with the unexpected. He hasn't cached anything in the area he's headed for because, chances are, he doesn't know where he's headed. Somehow, he hopes to overcome all odds with a minimum of supplies and a maximum of smarts. Certainly it is a noble cause; but it seems like one that is destined for failure."

Clearly, bugging out does not have many merits as a primary survival strategy in the event of any kind of major societal meltdown or economic collapse; however, there are times when "bugging out" makes real sense.

When Bugging Out Makes Sense

Bugging out makes sense in the context of a temporary evacuation.
If your home simply isn't going to be safe to live in after a natural disaster, then it makes sense to evacuate. In this case, your bug-out location could be as simple as a hotel three cities away. You obviously shouldn't stay and cling to your fortress home when it's about to be flooded. If your home has been flattened by an earthquake or a tornado you also don't want to stick around until it's safe to return to the area. Short-term situations involving a dangerous chemical or biological hazard might also necessitate bugging out. The seventy-two-hour bug-out bag is, in fact, ideally designed for these sorts of scenarios (which is why most good bug-out bags will include your most important papers, cash, and credit or debit cards—items that wouldn't help much in some of the Phase 3 or Phase 4 total meltdown scenarios). The bag ensures that you'll be okay for a few days if you get caught by the side of the road in with a car whose gas tank is stuck on empty, for example— just in case you can't ever make it to that hotel. (You don't want to risk going to shelters—shelters are quickly overwhelmed, run out of supplies, and wind up attracting criminals like flies in spite of the best efforts of the good people who open them and attempt to manage them).

Bugging out makes sense if you have somewhere else to go.
No, you haven't prepared a rural retreat, but you do have relatives and friends. You've gotten in touch with them, either long before the disaster or just after the disaster. They know you're coming and are all right with you doing so. They're willing to house you until you can fend for yourself (or for the foreseeable future in an arrangement where everyone is seeing to the security and prosperity of the home). In this case, you're not just becoming a hapless victim of the wilderness or a wandering refugee. You have a clear destination in mind, even in the event of a meltdown. Ideally you've plotted ways to get to that destination, whether via car or via any other form of transportation that may be functioning. If you have to

make it on foot, your bug-out bag at least gives you a better-than-average chance of being capable of doing so.

Bugging out makes sense if you have no choice.

Having that bug-out bag will be a godsend if you just don't have any other choice. If looters burn your home to the ground in spite of your best efforts to defend yourself, then you might have to slip out the back with nothing but your bag and your wits to embrace an uncertain destiny. If your home is facing impending nuclear winter from a nearby ground zero and there's no chance it will ever be safe to return during your lifetime, then yes, it's best to grab your bag and take your chances. If you are forcibly relocated from your home because some government thug says so, then you are, again, best served by having gear vital to your survival packed away in advance so you can grab and go without panic. If you wind up having to escape from martial law and you are relying on caches and escape routes to give you a fighting chance of evading capture, then you again, have no choice but to play "backpack survivalist" until a better situation unfolds (but at least in this scenario you know that you need to at least get to your escape and evasion cache and use it before plotting your next move). Just understand that at this point you become a refugee, and there are few more dangerous situations to find yourself in. It will take all of your wits, all of your skills, and the grace of God to see you through.

Building Your Bug-Out Bag

There are a lot of schools of thought to how to build a bug-out bag. Some of them involve using army-grade carrying racks that would allow you to lug twenty pounds of supplies through the wilderness. The problem with such bags is that they are destined to draw attention and make you a target for thieves. Bug-out bags which fit into small urban backpacks are probably a better bet for avoiding attention, even if it means giving up on a few items you'd rather have at your disposal. Each family member should have their own bag packed and ready to go.

Since your car, and not your feet, should be the first choice for any real travel you will also want to pack a "bug-out" kit for your car.[88] This kit is also useful to have in the event that you get stranded in your car for any reason.

Minimum Bug-Out Bag Contents

- Three-day supply of food
- Water purification tablets, or a water-purifying non-disposable water bottle
- First aid kits
- Water (distilled water packets such as those found in first aid kits pack well)
- An army blanket (folds and travels well)
- A tube tent (shelter for up to two people, folds and travels well)
- Emergency cash
- Emergency credit or debit cards
- Identification and important papers
- Hand crank radio
- Tarp
- A good knife

Solutions from Science offers a pre-made bug-out bag at www.myevacpack. com. This pack includes just about anything you'd need to have on hand; you'd simply need to add your cash, ID, and important papers. It would be good for each member of the family to have one—the redundancy can help you if you have to stay on the road or in the wild for longer than three days.

Minimum Car Bug-Out Kit Items

- A case of bottled water
- Blankets
- Flashlights and fresh batteries
- Signal flares
- Glow sticks
- First aid kit
- Food (crackers, beef jerky, energy bars, dried fruits, nuts, etc.)
- Emergency cash
- Toilet paper

The Best Bet

If urban locations are iffy, rural retreats are dangerous, and backpacking is a perilous latter of last resort, where should you be thinking about settling down and making investments in a fortress home? Is *anywhere* safe?

Fortunately, there is an answer, and it's delightfully simple. The small town offers real advantages to anyone who is concerned with their survival. In Argentina, people who lived in small towns have fared better than the isolated farmers and the city dwellers alike.89 Mel Tappan also noted the clear advantages of the small town:

> *"You can move [to a small town] now and live comfortably with whatever conveniences your means allow, for whatever period of grace we may have before the breakdown occurs, and by doing so, you can eliminate the two greatest risks of the survival equation: (1) estimating or recognizing the time when you should leave for your retreat and (2) the hazardous travel that might be involved in getting there when the crisis actually occurs."90*

Small towns, if you get there early enough to actually integrate yourself into the life of the town, offer a close-knit community of people who are more likely to run to your defense if someone is bothering you. They have the infrastructure, in fact, to potentially set up a town-wide defense as we discussed in previous chapters. They are likely to block off their roads and force people to move on in the event of a disaster, particularly if they are close to major cities, so you will need to be there *now*. Small towns surrounded by farming communities are likely to have farmers ready to come in to sell food, meaning you'll have access to food even if you don't have the green thumb to grow your own food. You'll have trustworthy people to barter with and a range of people with a range of skills to interact with. You'll be able to focus on turning your own skills to your best advantage and the best advantage of the community without spending loads of time and energy working on things that you have no aptitude for. You should still fortify your home—you won't be immune to all troubles—but the chances that help is on the way will be far greater. A community of about 2,000-5,000 people is about right. Any smaller and you may have trouble integrating; any larger and you start inviting the problems of the big city right back onto your doorstep.

Once you get into the community, you'll want to start getting to know people. Joining the Neighborhood Watch or other crime fighting initiative would be helpful. So is going to church, showing up at community events, being active in your child's school, or joining any other club or organization. Be someone the community actually knows and cares about rather than someone who blew into town three days before disaster hit.

There are millions of these towns in the United States. If you still need to work in a city, you can find one close enough to commute to (just know your escape routes if you need to get back to your small town home on foot). If you work from home or have a profession that easily translates nearly anywhere, it's possible you may be able to simply find a job in one of these communities. You can then enjoy all the normal comforts of modern living for as long as possible—from grocery stores to movie theatres—knowing that you've given yourself a "best bet" situation. Having a fortress matters little if it's in an inauspicious location. Remaining in the city proper carries its own dangers (though yes, it is possible to survive even in cities); rural locations carry their own danger—small towns offer the "just right" solution to the problem.

CONCLUSION

Conclusion

ഇ•ൽ

The purpose of preparedness is neither fear nor paranoia. It's a matter of personal responsibility—of soberly weighing trends and historic patterns to arrive at some conclusions about the sort of world you're likely to be living in during the near future. That is why we've taken the time to show you case studies from real places and historic events—to show you the reasons why preparing for the coming crime nightmare just makes sense personally and financially.

I urge you to soberly consider all of the information we've presented here—to understand the way the crime nightmare is likely to impact you and your family. Even the early stages of the nightmare are extremely dangerous—the world need never progress to some of the worst cases to make fortifying your home make a great deal of sense.

Yet all of the information in the world will not matter if you don't start taking some action. Start small and build your way up to the highest degree of readiness over time. Just don't take too much time. The situation is growing worse by the day, with no end in sight. Day by day we are waking up to a very different America, and we'll be feeling the effect of all of the mistakes that led us to this point even if we all managed to turn around and change course tomorrow. Pray, survive, and work to make a better future for your children and grandchildren.

Endnotes

1. Lockjaw Security. Lockjaw Security. [Online] [Cited: 5 27, 2011.] http://www.lockjawsecurity.com/pdf/LockBumpingFactSheet.pdf.
2. Big Dogs and 7 Other Ineffective Burglar Deterrents. *Apartment Therapy.* [Online] 2008. [Cited: 5 31, 2011.] http://www.apartmenttherapy.com/chicago/security/big-dogs-and-7-other-ineffective-burglar-deterrentsbottom-line-summer-2008-054581.
3. KTVU: Search on for Suspect in Brutal Home Invasion. *KTVU.* [Online] KTVU, 5 27, 2011. [Cited: 5 27, 2011.] http://www.ktvu.com/news/28048439/detail.html.
4. Herald Online: 2 Arrested After Clover Home Invasion, Fatal Shooting. *Herald Online.* [Online] The Herald, 5 27, 2011. [Cited: 5 27, 2011.] http://www.heraldonline.com/2011/05/27/3103375/2-charged-after-clover-home-invasion.html.
5. Columbus Dispatch. *Columbus Dispatched: Rapist Senteced to 33 Years.* [Online] Columbus Dispatch, 5 25, 2011. [Cited: 5 27, 2011.] http://www.dispatch.com/live/content/local_news/stories/2011/05/25/rapist-sentenced-to-33-years.html?sid=101.
6. DIY Window Security. *DIY Window Security.* [Online] DIY Window Security, 2010. [Cited: 5 25, 2011.] http://www.diywindowsecurity.com/smash-and-grab.php?osCsid=3b6b3d3f143309b7b304bfcdd107adcd.
7. The Flint Journal. The Flint Journal: Dangling Toys Pose Mystery on Flint's East Side. *MLive.com.* [Online] The Flint Journal, 1 21, 2011. [Cited: 6 7, 2011.] http://www.mlive.com/news/flint/index.ssf/2011/01/dangling_toys_pose_mystery_on.html.
8. Crow, Carl. *The City of Flint Grows Up.* New York: Harper & Brothers, 1945.
9. The Flint Journal: Flint Homicides This Year Surpassing Pace of

Record 2010. *MLive.Com.* [Online] The Flint Journal, 5 27, 2011. [Cited: 6 7, 2011.] http://www.mlive.com/news/flint/index.ssf/2011/05/flint_homicides_this_year_surp.html.

10. Wes Janz, PhD, RA. *Deconstructing Flint.* Muncie, Indiana: Report Submitted to Genesee Institute, Genesee County Land Bank, 2007.

11. New York Times: An Effort to Save Flint, Mich. by Shrinking It. *The New York Times.* [Online] The New York , 4 22, 2009. [Cited: 6 7, 2011.] http://www.nytimes.com/2009/04/22/business/22flint.html.

12. Ibid, 8.

13. Elliot, Larry. US Unemployment Unacceptably High, White House Advisors Admit. *The London Guardian.* [Online] The London Guardian, 6 3, 2011. [Cited: 6 7, 2011.] http://www.guardian.co.uk/business/2011/jun/03/us-nonfarm-payrolls-unemployment-white-house.

14. Real U.S. unemployment rate may be 22.1 percent for February. *The European Union Times.* [Online] The EU Times, 3 6, 2011. [Cited: 6 7, 2011.] http://www.eutimes.net/2011/03/real-us-unemployment-rate-may-be-22-percent-for-february/.

15. Wessel, David. Big U.S. Firms Shift Hiring Abroad: Work Forces Shrink at Home, Sharpening Debate on the Economic Impact of Globalization. *The Wall Street Journal.* [Online] The Wall Street Journal, 4 19, 2011. [Cited: 6 8, 2011.] http://online.wsj.com/article/SB10001424052748704576270783611823972.html.

16. Revzin, Eric Pooley and Philip. Hungry for a Solution to Rising Food Prices: Even if the Global Agriculture Crisis Doesn't Turn Cataclysmic, It Represents a Massive Test. *Bloomberg Businessweek.* [Online] Bloomberg, 2 17, 2011. [Cited: 6 8, 2011.] http://www.businessweek.com/magazine/content/11_09/b4217007869373.htm.

17. Ohio State University. Research News. *Research News.* [Online] Research News. [Cited: 7 2011, 6.] researchnews.osu.edu/archive//crimwage.htm.

18. Baker, Christine Hauser and Al. Keeping a Wary Eye on Crime As Economy Sinks. *The New York Times.* [Online] The New York Times, 10 9, 2008. [Cited: 8 2011, 6.] http://www.nytimes.com/2008/10/10/nyregion/10crime.html.

19. *Trends Journal Top Trends of 2011.* Celente, Gerald. s.l.: The Trends Research Institute, 2011.

20. Mackey, Judge Alfred. *Judge Tells Residents to Arm Themselves.* s.l.: NBC WKYC, 4 9, 2010.

21. NPR. Sheriff to Texas Border Town: Arm Yourselves. *NPR.* [Online] NPR, 4 9, 2010. [Cited: 6 15, 2911.] http://www.npr.org/templates/story/story.php?storyId=125737965.

22. Johnson, Kevin. Police Training Halts as Agencies Face Budget Cuts. *USA Today.* [Online] USA Today, 10 4, 2010. [Cited: 6 15, 2011.] www.usatoady.com/news/nation/2010-10-04-cop-training-n.htm.

23. Thoughts on Urban Survival: Life in Post-Collapse Argentina. [book auth.] Greg Evenson. *The Big Red Castle Defense Manual.*

24. Rawles, James Wesley. The Precepts of Rawlesian Survivalist Philosophy.

25. Ibid, 23.

26. SurviveInPlace.com. The Will to Survive. [book auth.] Greg Evanson. *The Big Red Castle Defense Manual.*

27. Ibid, 23.

28. Ibid, 23.

29. Safe Room. *No Nonsense Self Defense.* [Online] [Cited: 6 16, 2011.] http://www.nononsenseselfdefense.com/saferoom.htm.

30. Ibid, 29.

31. Ibid, 29.

32. Ibid, 30.

33. Adams, Sam. *Hide Your Guns.* Thomson, IL: Solutions from Science, 2008.

34. Ibid, 33.

35. Ibid, 33.
36. Aguirre, Fernando. Police Corruption. *Surviving in Argentina.* [Online] 8 2, 2010. [Cited: 6 24, 2011.] ferfal.blogspot.com/search/label/Security.
37. Ibid, 36.
38. Ibid, 23.
39. Cisneros, Henry. *Defensible Space: Deterring Crime and Building Community.* 1995.
40. Seattle Police Department. Crime Prevention. *Seattle Police Website.* [Online] Seattle Police Department. [Cited: 6 24, 2011.] www.ci.seattle.wa.us/police/prevention/Neighborhood/brokenwindow.htm.
41. National Youth Network, Youth in Action. Youth In Action, July 1999, Number 9. *NCJrs.Gov.* [Online] US Department of Justice, 7 1999. [Cited: 6 24, 2011.] www.ncjrs.gov/pdffiles/1781690.pdf.
42. Sacramento County Sheriff's Department. Citizens Against Crime. *Sacramento County Sheriff's Department.* [Online] Sacramento County Sheriff's Department. [Cited: 6 24, 2011.] www.sacsheriff.com/crime_prevention/documents/neighborhood_watch_06.cfm.
43. Ibid, 42.
44. Shumand, Greg Evensen and Rick. *The Castle Defense 2.* Heartland USA, 2009.
45. Pirovolakis, David Williams and Christine. Athens Alight: Thousands of Striking Greeks in Fresh Anti-Cut Riot...and This is Them Just Warming Up for Clashes Tomorrow. *Mail Online.* [Online] Mail Online, 28 2011, 6. [Cited: 28 2011, 6.] http://www.dailymail.co.uk/news/article-2008905/Greek-vote-Protests-Athens-MPs-debate-EUs-25bn-cuts.html.
46. Wood, Daniel B. LA's Darkest Days. *The Christian Science Monitor.* [Online] The Christian Science Monitor, 4 29, 2002. [Cited: 6 28, 2011.] http://www.csmonitor.com/2002/0429/p01s07-ussc.html.

47. CNN. A Freenzy of Looting Seen In Haiti. *CNN World.* [Online] CNN, 1 18, 2010. [Cited: 6 28, 2011.] http://articles.cnn.com/2010-01-18/world/haiti.looting.earthquake_1_looting-haiti-s-capital-security-council?_s=PM:WORLD.

48. Frayer, Lauren. Why Is There No Looting in Japan in Earthquake Aftermath. *AOL World.* [Online] AOL, 3 16, 2011. [Cited: 6 29, 2011.] http://www.aolnews.com/2011/03/16/why-is-there-no-looting-in-japan-in-earthquake-aftermath/.

49. Rawles, James Wesley. Riots and Civil Unrest in America by B.B. in California. *Survival Blog.* [Online] 7 21, 2010. [Cited: 6 28, 2011.] www.survivalblog.com/2010/07/riots_and_civil_unrest_in_amer.html.

50. Saever, Philip Sherwell and Patrick. Haiti Earthquake: Looting and Gun-Fights Break Out. *The London Telegraph.* [Online] The Telegraph, 1 16, 2010. [Cited: 6 28, 2011.] http://www.telegraph.co.uk/news/worldnews/centralamericaandthecaribbean/haiti/7005554/Haiti-earthquake-looting-and-gun-fights-break-out.html.

51. Upi.Com. Missouri Tornado Victims Suffer Looting. *Upi.Com.* [Online] Upi.com, 6 23, 2011. [Cited: 6 28, 2011.] www.upi.com/Top_News/US/2011/06/23/missouri_tornado_victims_suffer_looting/upi_62914308860935.

52. WCVBS TV 5 Boston. Tornado Victims Fight Off Looters With Crowbars. *WCVB TV 5 Boston.* [Online] ABC, 3 6, 2011. [Cited: 6 28, 2011.] www.thebostonchannel.com/+128126702/detail.html.

53. Ibid, 38.

54. Solutions from Science. Your Fortress Home. *Off the Grid News: Better Ideas for Off the Grid Living.* [Online] Solutions from Science, 8 9, 2010. [Cited: 6 25, 2011.] www.offthegridnews.com/2010/08/09/your-fortress-home/.

55. Ibid, 38.

56. Ibid, 46.

57. Ibid, 46.

58. Ibid, 46.

59. Buckley, J. Patrick. Booby Traps are Never Legal. *NaplesNews.com.* [Online] 5 15, 2010. [Cited: 6 25, 2011.] blogs.naplesnews.com/florida-law/2010/05/boobytraps-are-never-legal.html.

60. Morriss, David. Survive in Place Lesson 13. *Survive in Place.* [Online] [Cited: 25 2011, 6.] surviveinplace.com.

61. United States Army. *FM Reprinted 21-76 US Army Survival Manual.* s.l.: US Army.

62. Ibid, 53.

63. Ibid, 33.

64. City of Sugar Land. Avoid Being Followed Home. *City of Sugar Land, TX.* [Online] City of Sugar Land. [Cited: 6 27, 2011.] www.sugarlandtx.gov/police/services/crime_prevention/.

65. Creekmore, M.D. Why Aren't You Raising an Emergency Garden? *The Survivalist Blog.* [Online] www.thesurvivalistblog.net, 2011. [Cited: 6 27, 2011.] http://www.thesurvivalistblog.net/guerrilla-gardening/.

66. Ibid, 57.

67. Morris, David. Survive in Place Lesson 1. *Survive in Place Lesson 1.* s.l.: David Morris, 2009. Vol. 1.

68. Your Home Crisis Guidebook for a Survival Situation or SHTF. *Suburban Survival Blog.* [Online] [Cited: 6 29, 2011.] http://suburbansurvivalblog.com/your-home-crisis-guidebook-for-a-survival-situation-or-a-shtf.

69. Family Survival Kid's Disaster Kits. *SurvivalCache.com.* [Online] [Cited: 6 30, 2011.] www.survivalcache.com/family-survival-kids-disaster-kits-survival-supplies/.

70. Ibid, 69.

71. University of Illinois. Helping Children Cope With A Disaster. *University of Illinois Disaster Resources.* [Online] University of

Illinois. [Cited: 6 30, 2011.] http://web.extension.illinois.edu/disaster/facts/kidcope.html.

72. Ibid, 71.

73. FBI. FBI Joint Terrorism Task Force Pamphlet. [Online] [Cited: 7 2, 2011.] www.retakingamerica.com/files/fbi_flyer.pdf.

74. MIAC. MIAC Report Adds Opposition. [Online] [Cited: 7 2, 2011.] www.scribd.com/doc/13290698/The-Modern-Militia-MovementMissouri-MIAC-strategic-Report-20Feb09-.

75. Arkin, Dana Priest and William M. Monitoring America. [Online] The Washington Post, 2009. [Cited: 7 2, 2011.] http://projects.washingtonpost.com/top-secret-america/articles/monitoring-america.

76. Ibid, 75.

77. Life During Martial Law (Oral History, Mr. Siasat). *Clark Humanities*. [Online] 2006. [Cited: 7 2, 2011.] www.clarkhumanities.org/oralhistory/2006/2484.htm.

78. Harvey, Rachel. Life Under Martial Law in Aceh. *BBC News*. [Online] BBC News, 12 29, 2003. [Cited: 7 2, 2011.] news.bbc.co.uk/2/hi/asia-pacific/3353849.stm.

79. Adams, Sam. *Understanding and Surviving Martial Law*. Thomson: Solutions from Science, 2009.

80. Ibid, 79.

81. Ibid, 33.

82. Ibid, 33.

83. Ibid, 24.

84. Aguirre, Fernando. Home Invasion: Country vs. City after the Economic Collapse. *Surviving in Argentina*. [Online] 6 5, 2011. [Cited: 7 2, 2011.] http://ferfal.blogspot.com/2011/06/home-invasion-country-vs-city-after.html.

85. Tappan, Mel. Tappan on Survival (Book Reprint). *Tappan on Survival*. [Online] 1989. [Cited: 7 2, 2011.] www.giltweasal.com/stuff/Tapan%20

on%20survival.pdf.

86. Morris, David. Survive in Place. *Survive in Place.* [Online] [Cited: 7 2, 2011.] www.surviveinplace.com.

87. Long, Duncan. Backpack Fever. *American Survival Guide.* 1989.

88. Solutions From Science. *Gone Before You Get There: 77 Items That Instantly Vanish From Store Shelves in a Panic and Why Preparing For a Crisis Cannot Wait.* Thomson: Solutions From Science.

89. Ibid, 23.

90. Ibid, 85.

91. Ibid, 28.

92. Ibid, 38.

‍ℰꙄ•ℭ℞